What we Don't Talk About

Charlot Kristensen

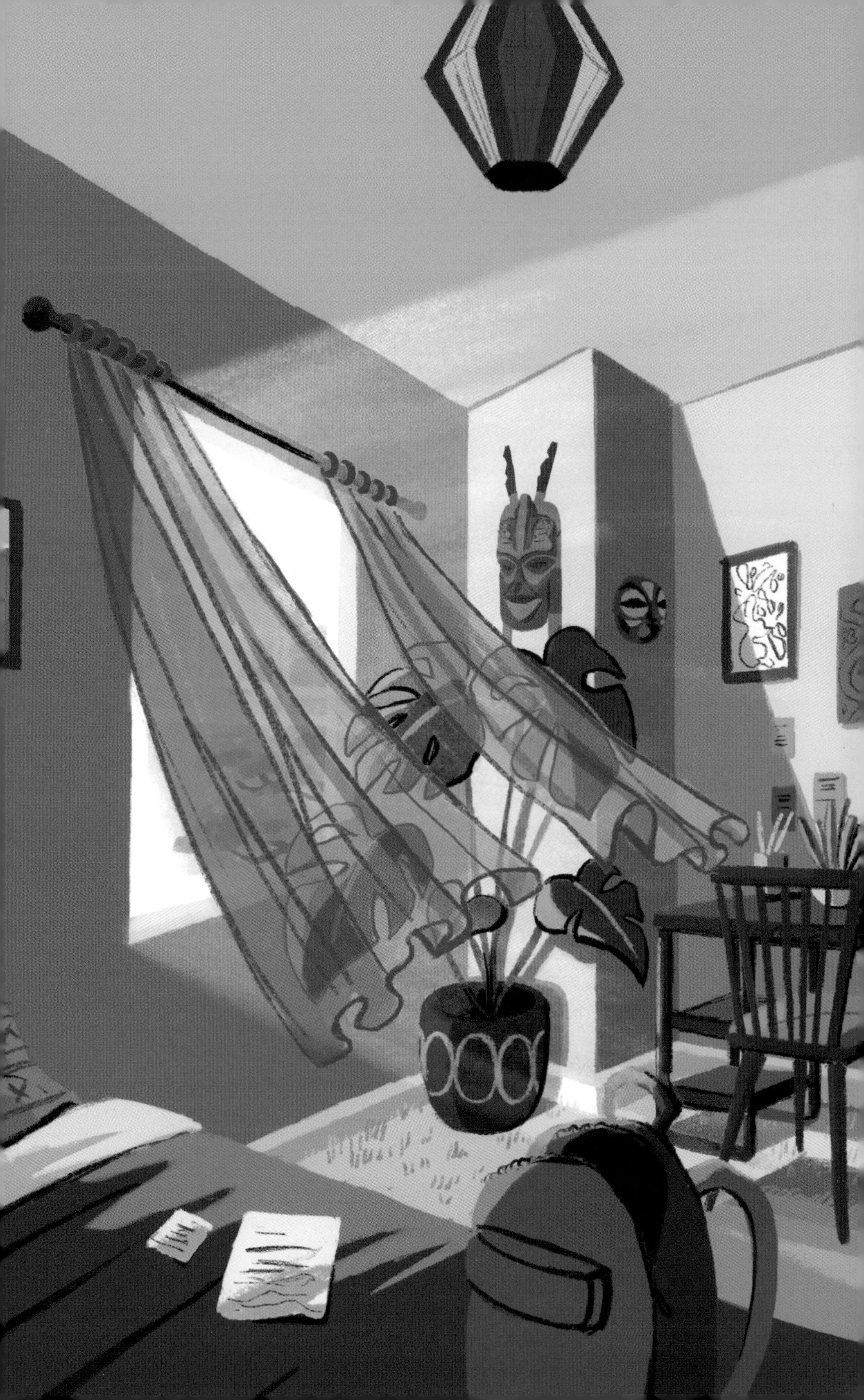

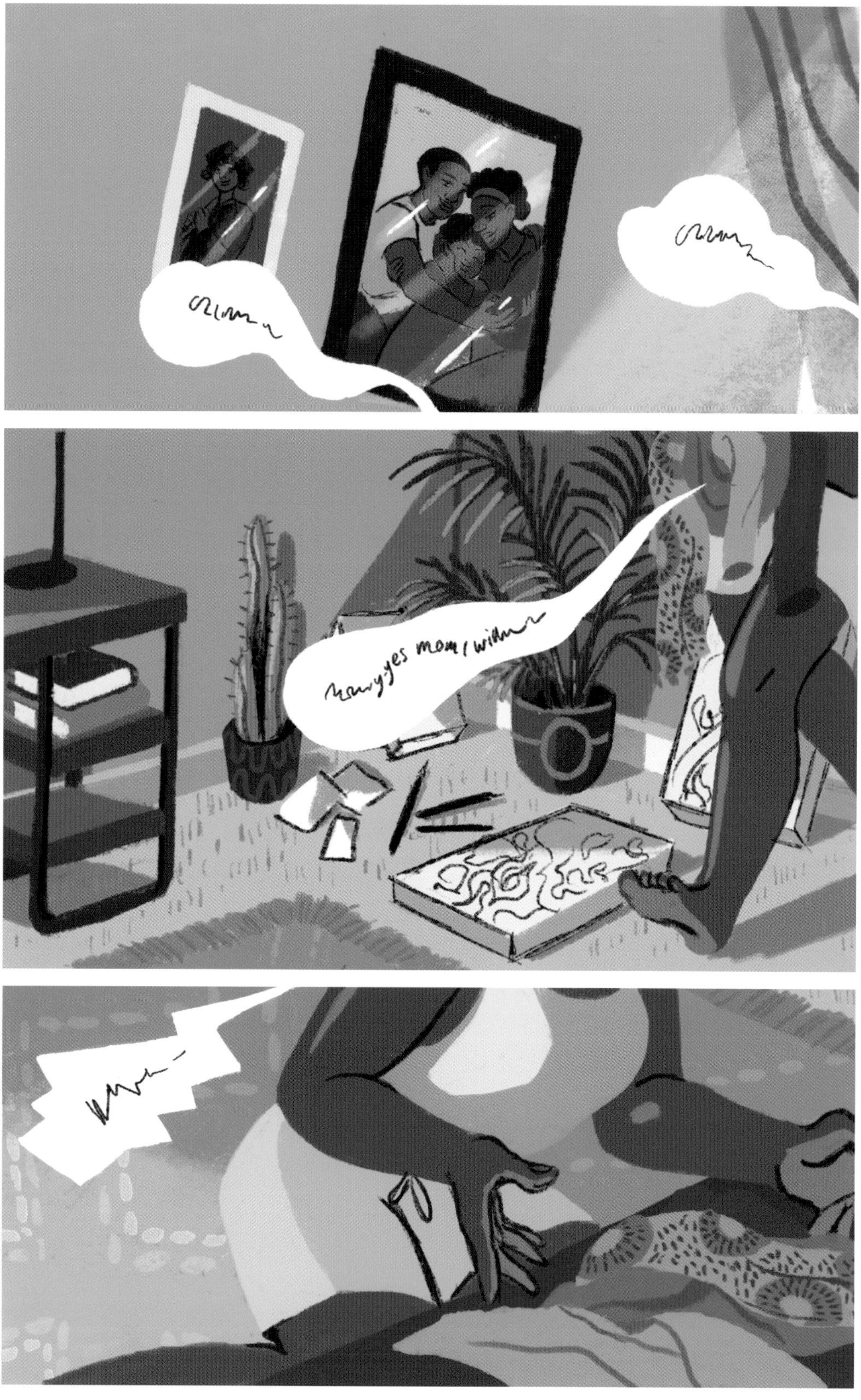
yes mom

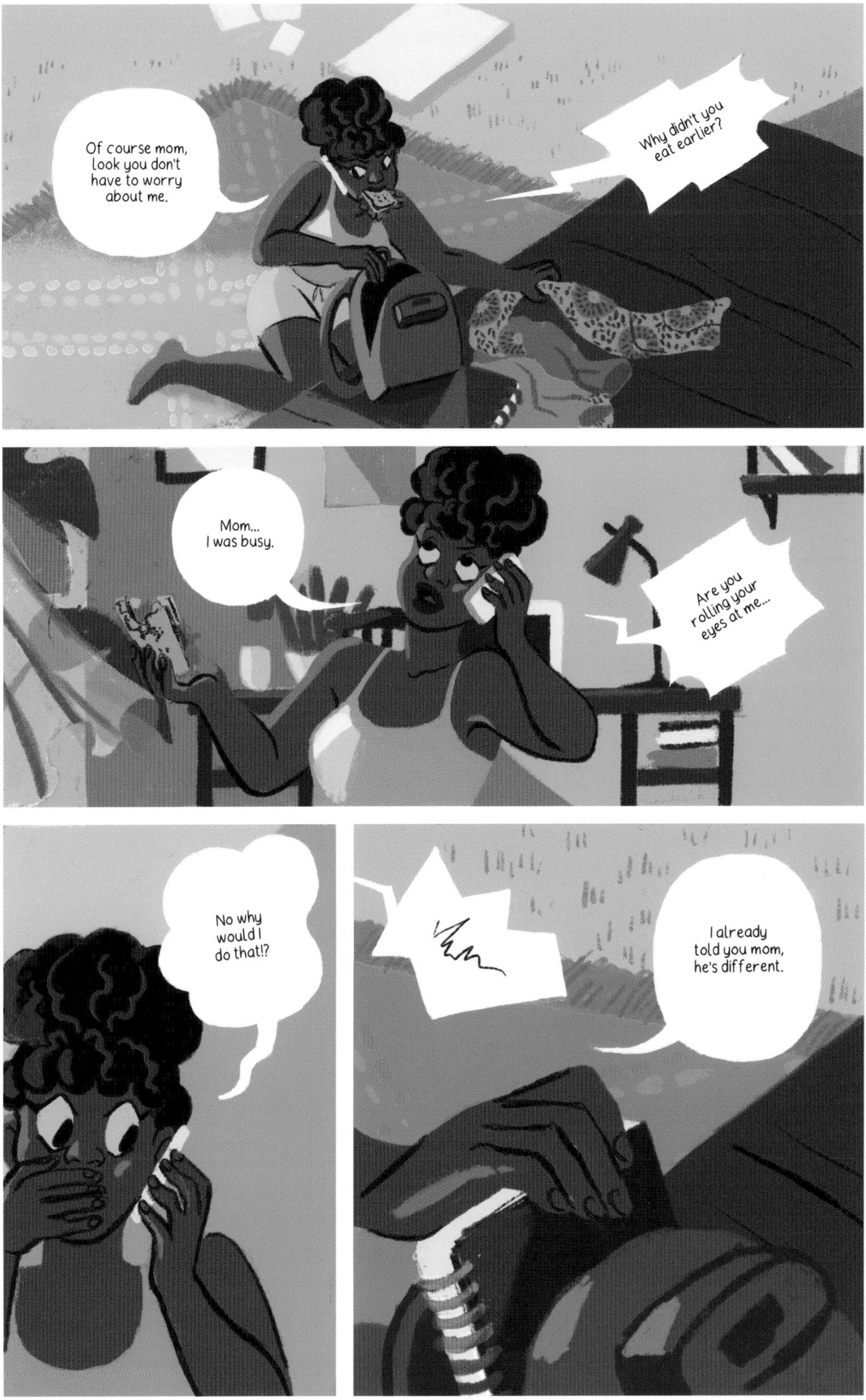
Of course mom, look you don't have to worry about me.
Why didn't you eat earlier?
Mom... I was busy.
Are you rolling your eyes at me...
No why would I do that!?
I already told you mom, he's different.

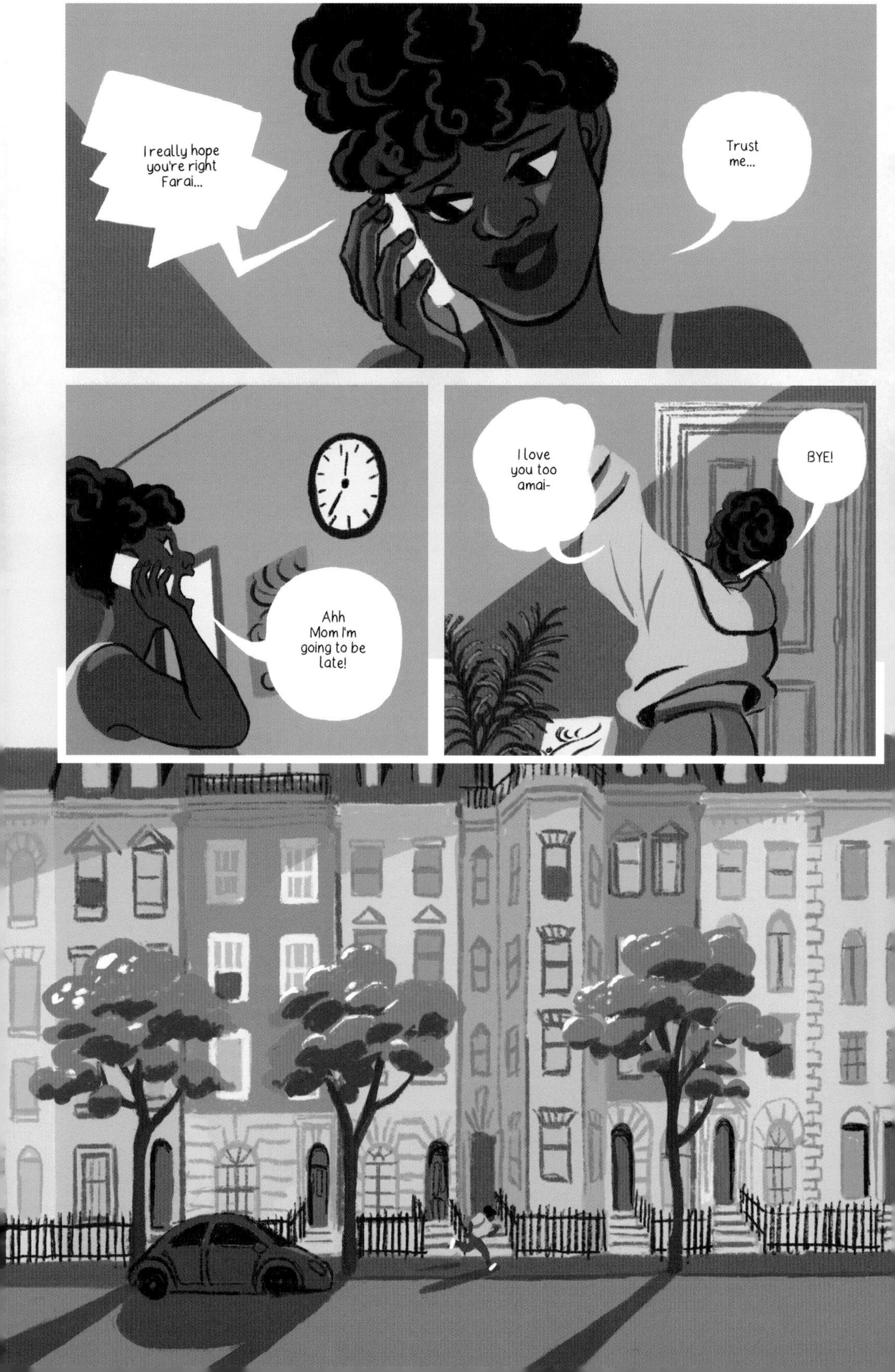
I really hope you're right Farai...
Trust me...
Ahh Mom I'm going to be late!
I love you too amai-
BYE!

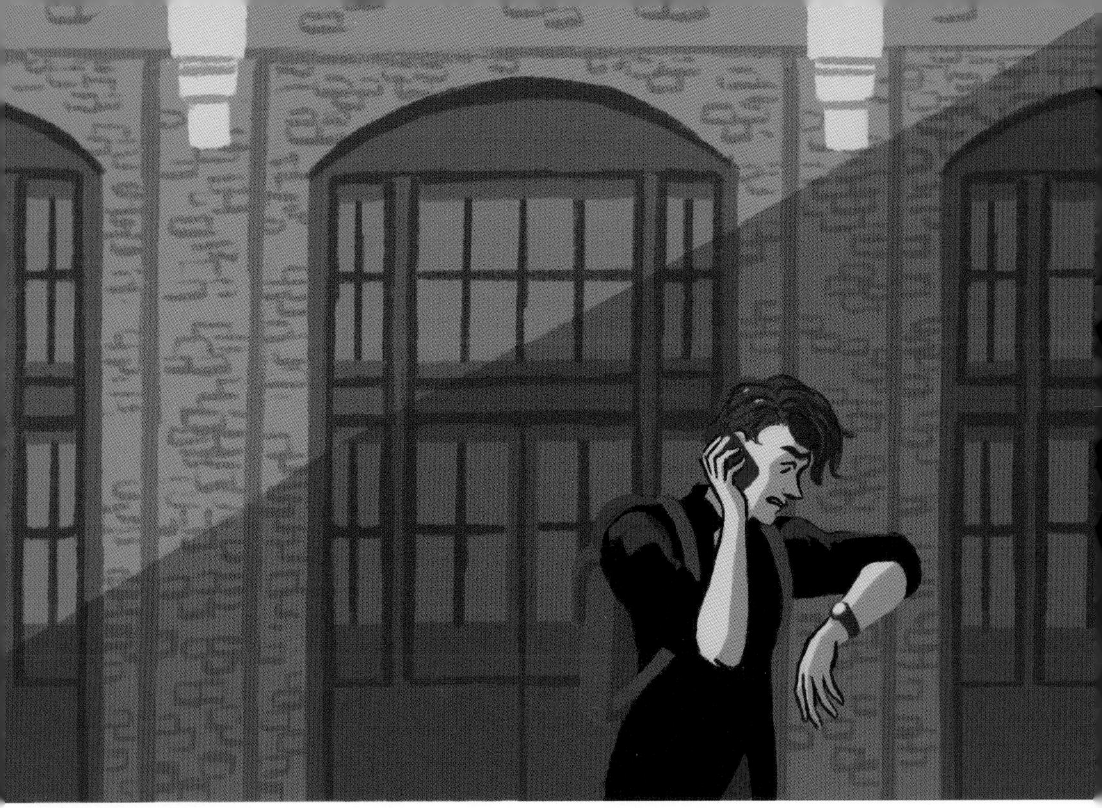

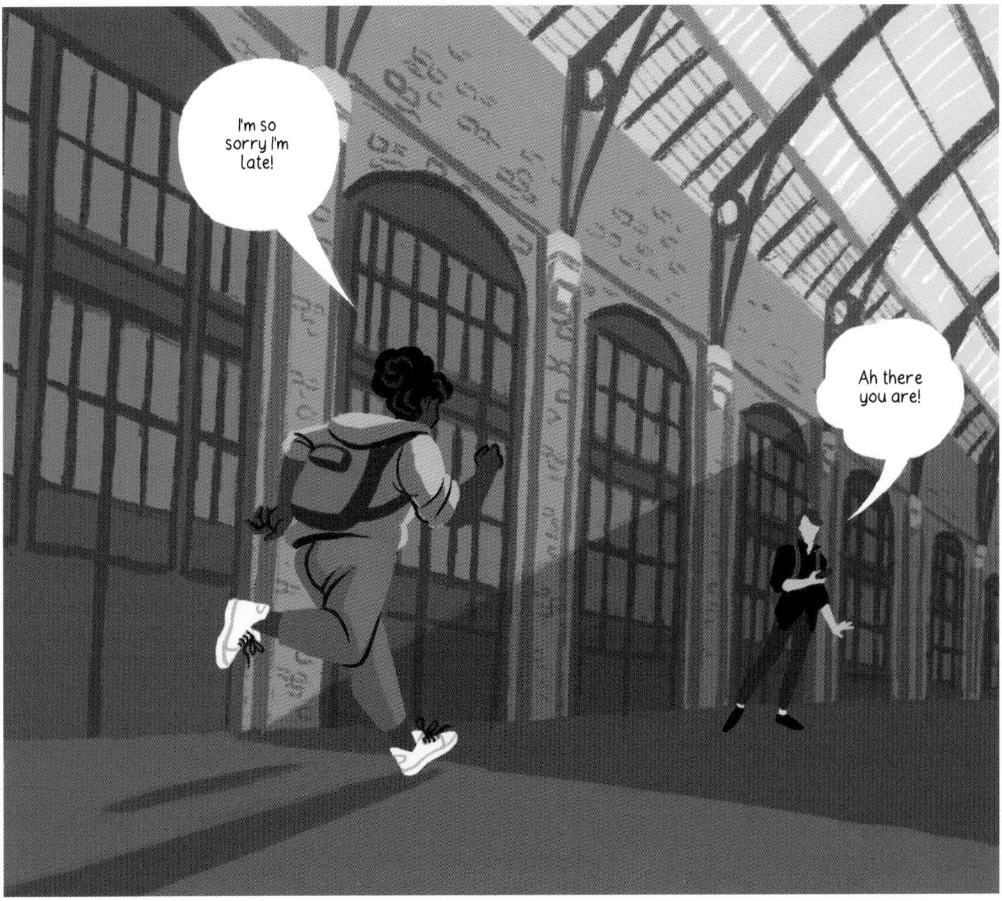
I'm so sorry I'm late!
Ah there you are!

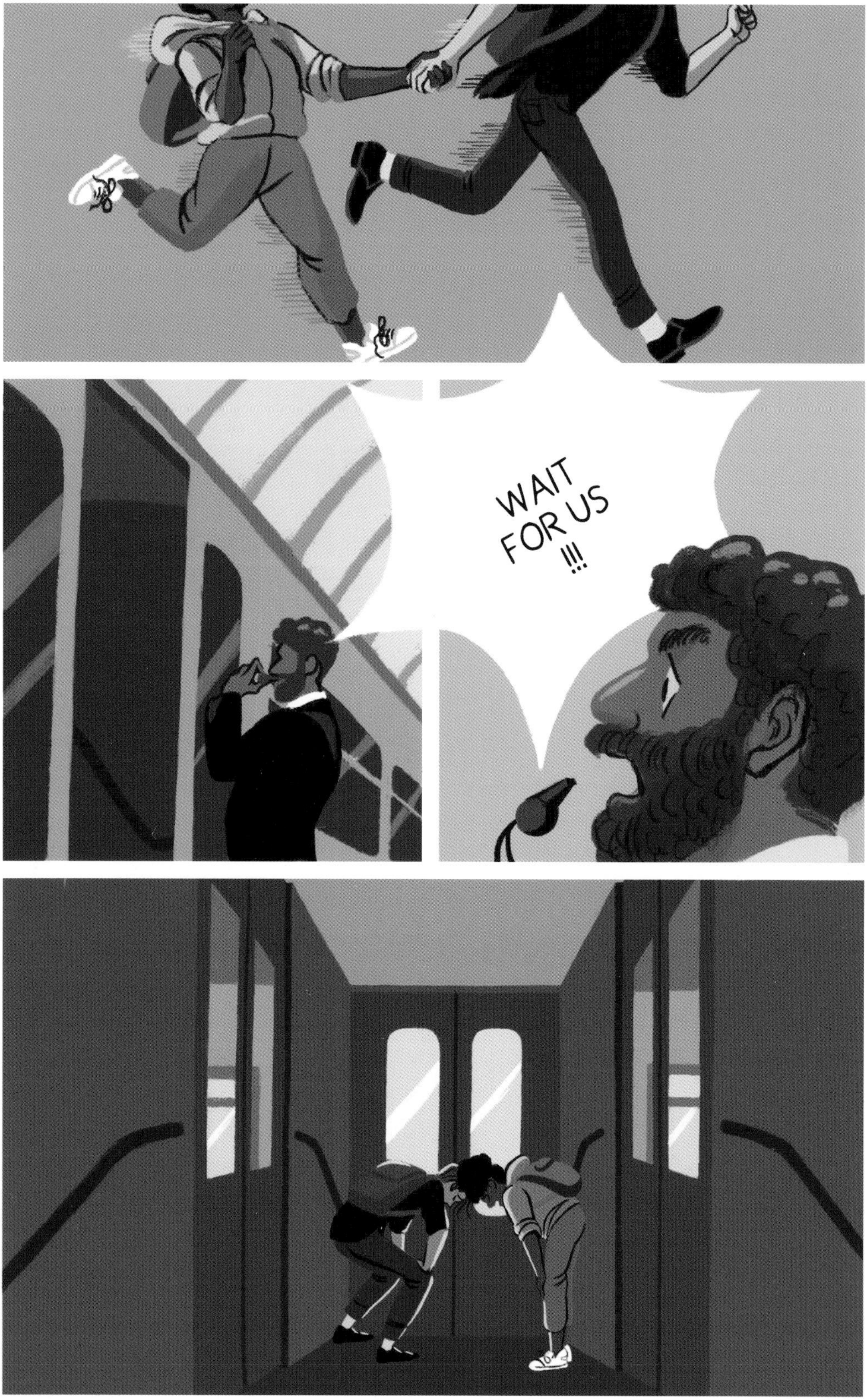
WAIT FOR US !!!

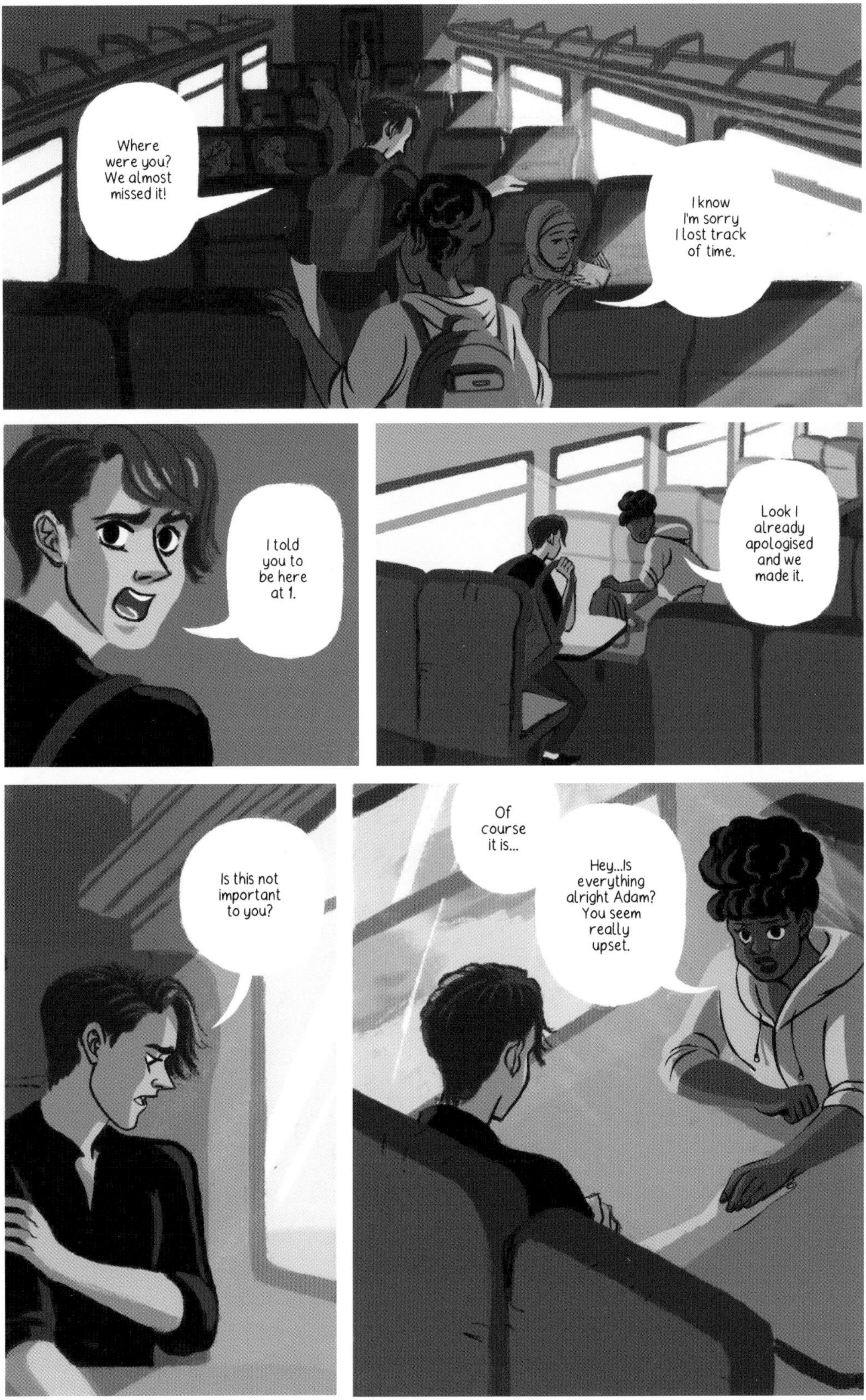
Where were you? We almost missed it!
I know I'm sorry I lost track of time.
I told you to be here at 1.
Look I already apologised and we made it.
Is this not important to you?
Of course it is...
Hey...Is everything alright Adam? You seem really upset.

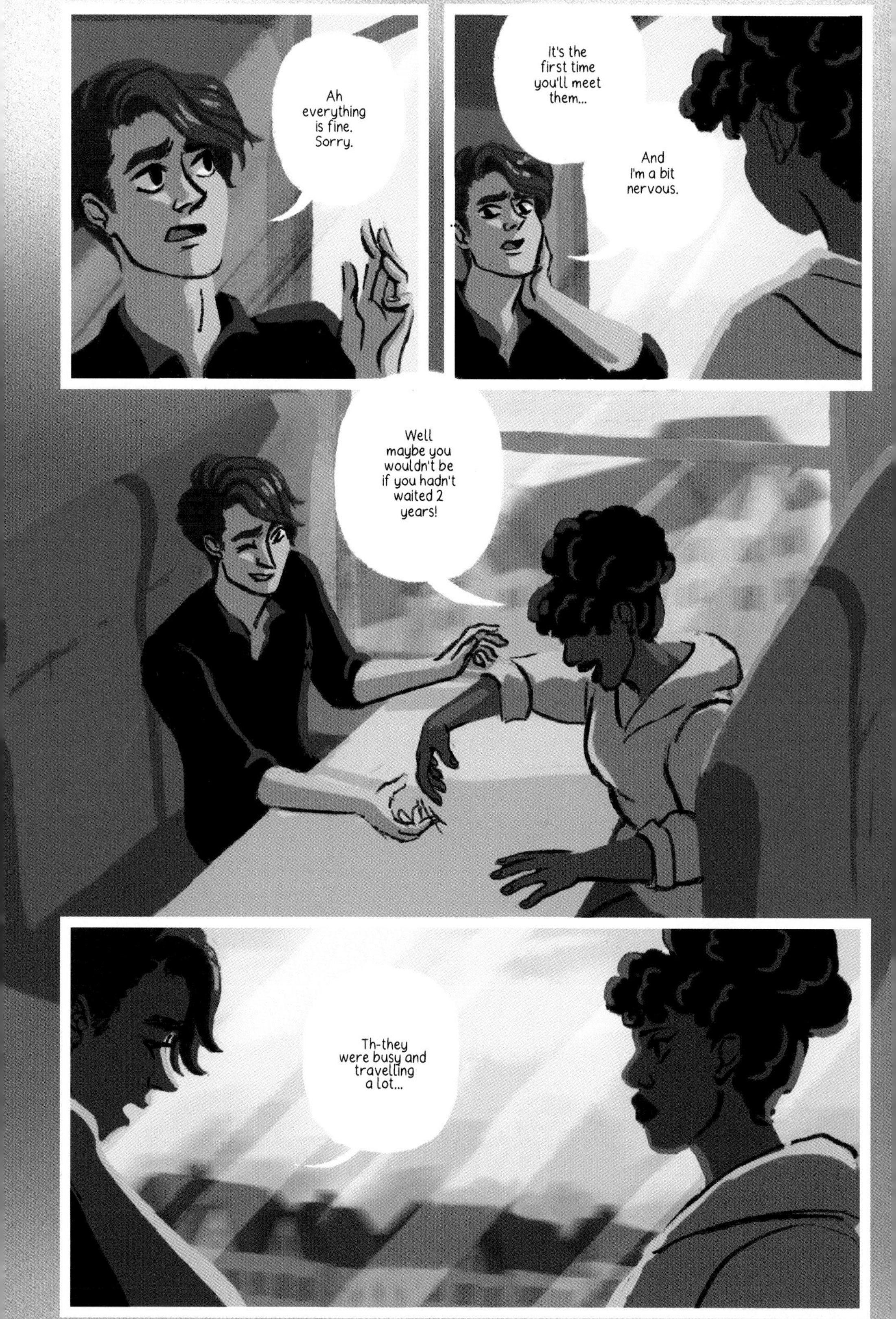
Ah everything is fine. Sorry.
It's the first time you'll meet them...
And I'm a bit nervous.
Well maybe you wouldn't be if you hadn't waited 2 years!
Th-they were busy and travelling a lot...

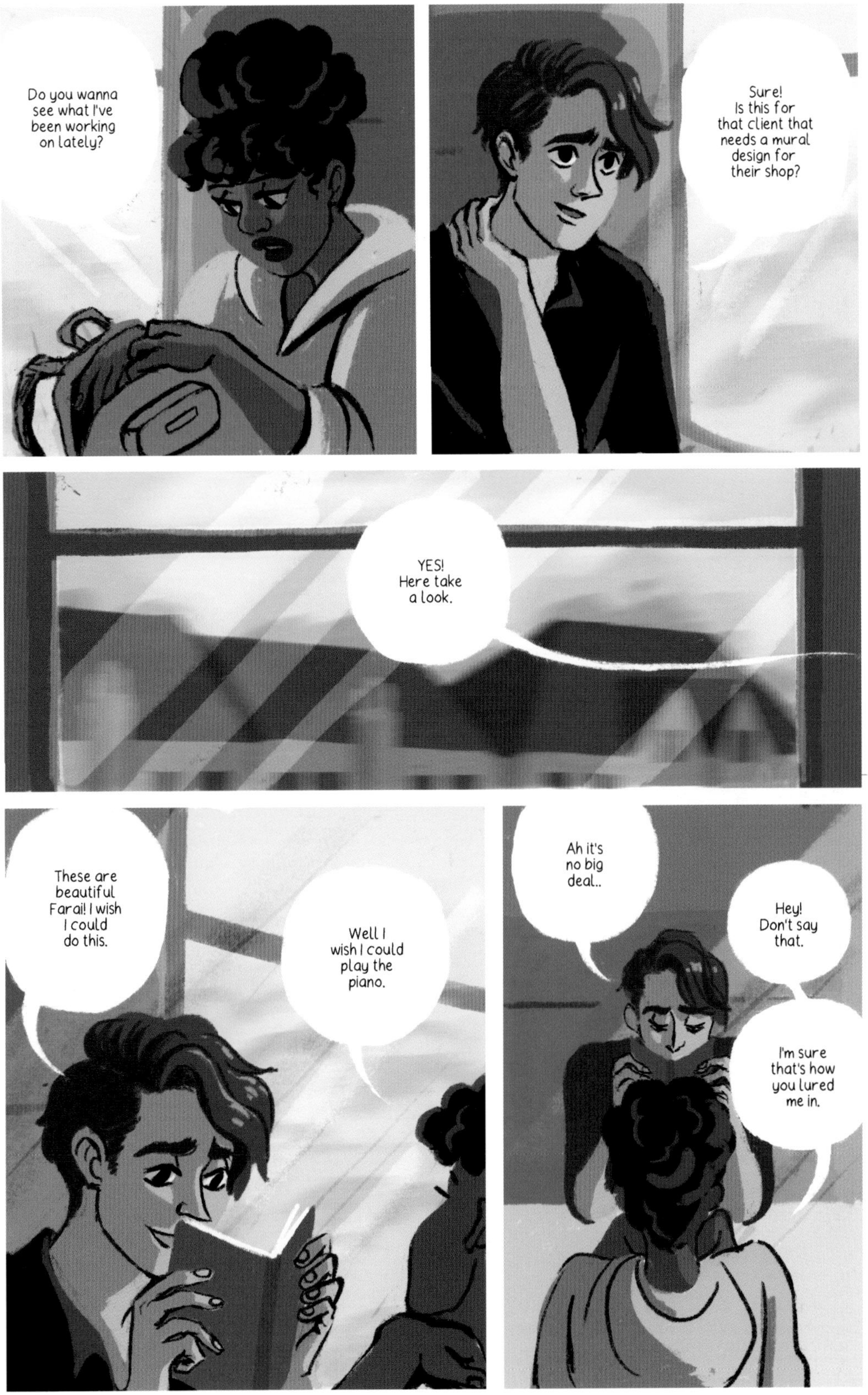
Do you wanna see what I've been working on lately?
Sure! Is this for that client that needs a mural design for their shop?
YES! Here take a look.
These are beautiful Farai! I wish I could do this.
Well I wish I could play the piano.
Ah it's no big deal..
Hey! Don't say that.
I'm sure that's how you lured me in.

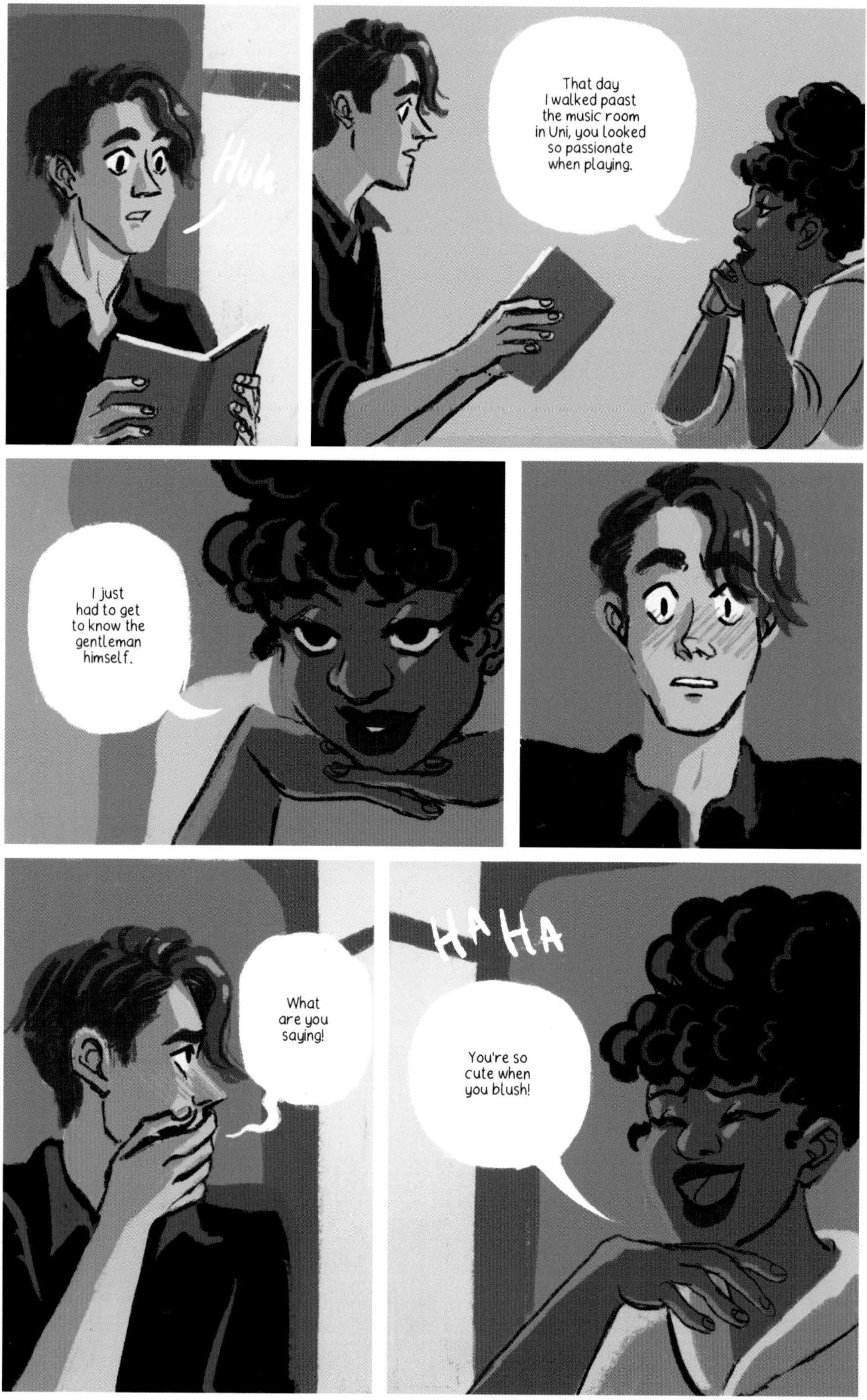
Huh
That day I walked paast the music room in Uni, you looked so passionate when playing.
I just had to get to know the gentleman himself.
What are you saying!
HA HA HA
You're so cute when you blush!

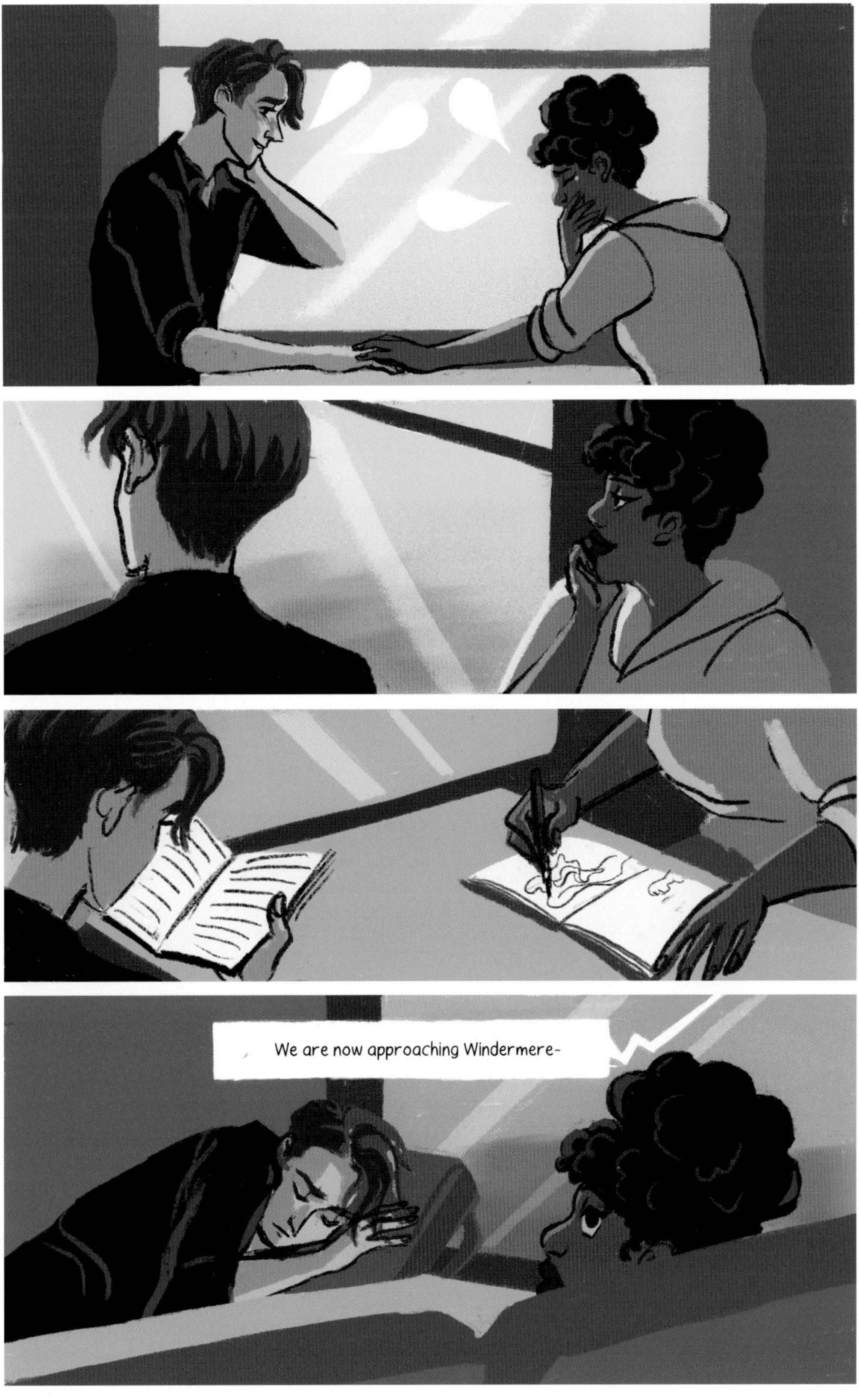
We are now approaching Windermere-

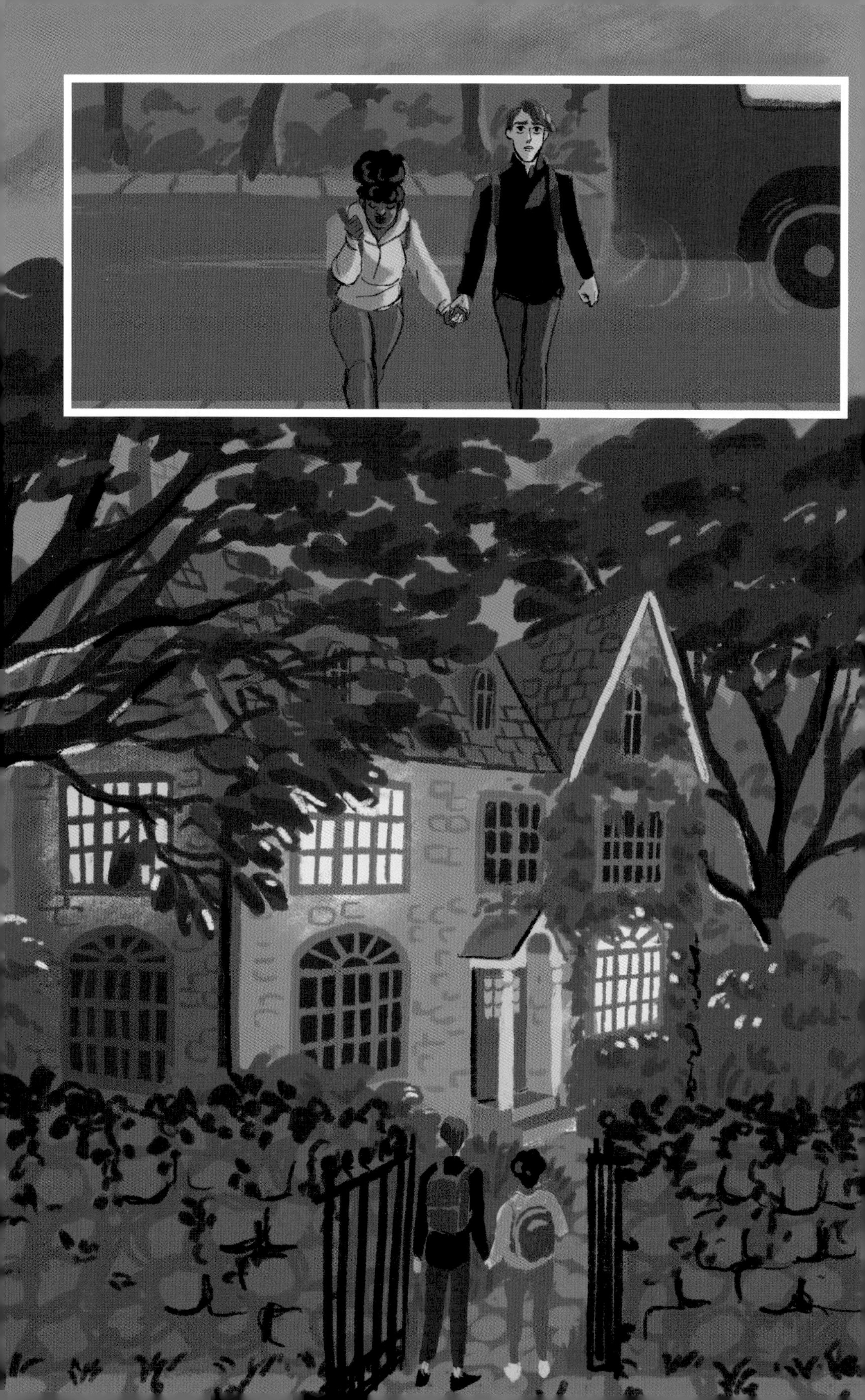

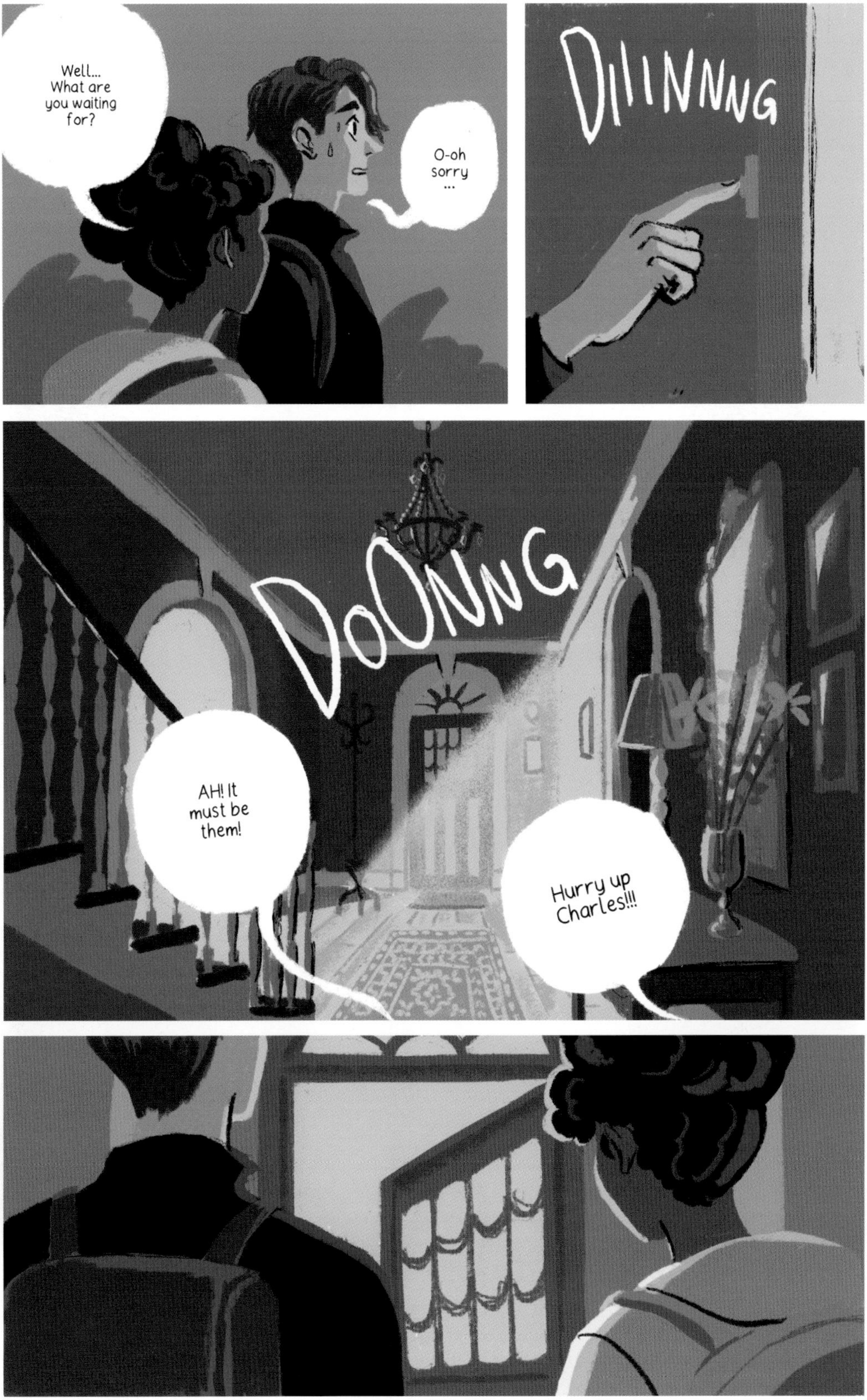
Well... What are you waiting for?
O-oh sorry ...
DIIINNNG
DOONNG
AH! It must be them!
Hurry up Charles!!!

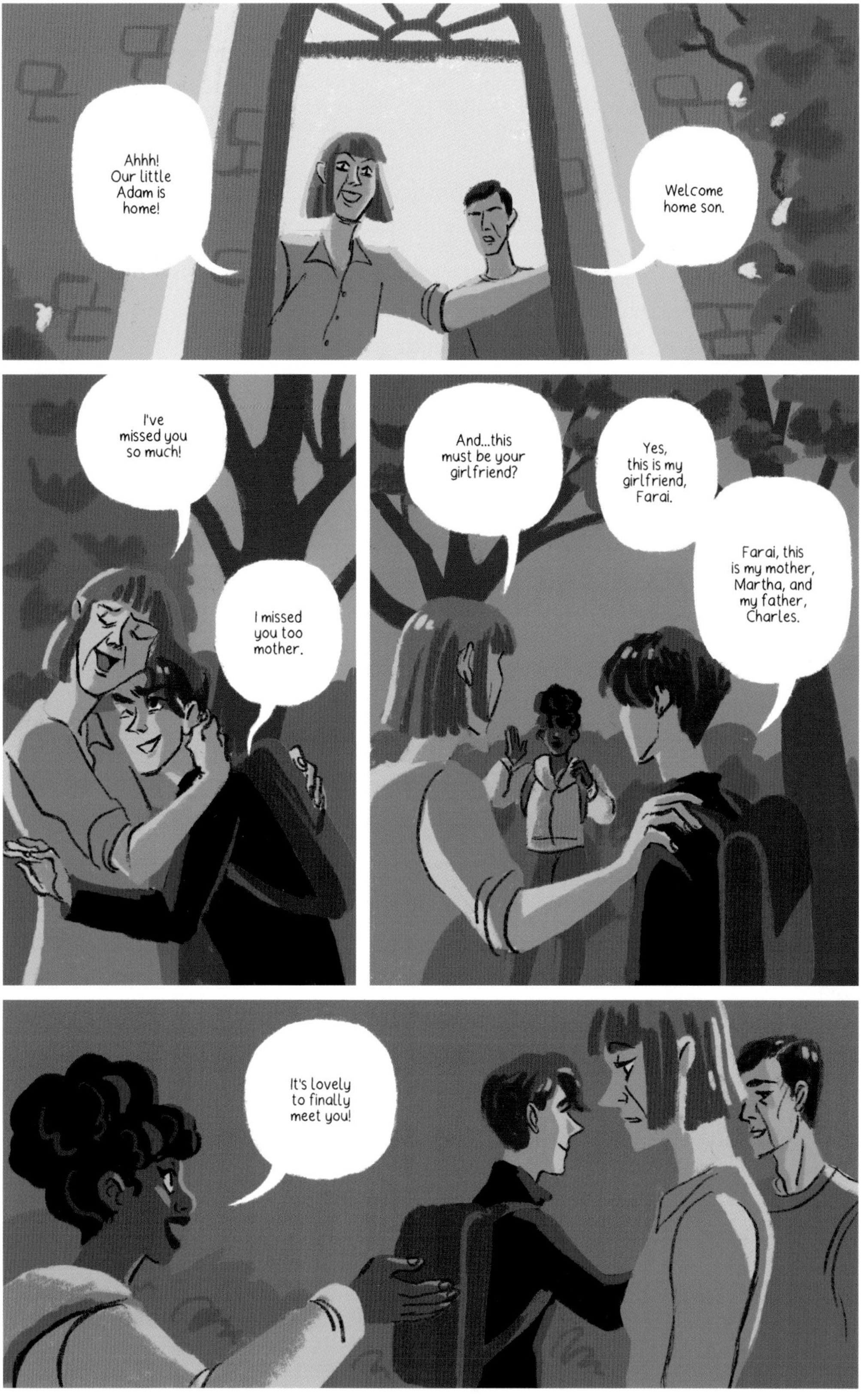
Ahhh! Our little Adam is home!
Welcome home son.
I've missed you so much!
I missed you too mother.
And...this must be your girlfriend?
Yes, this is my girlfriend, Farai.
Farai, this is my mother, Martha, and my father, Charles.
It's lovely to finally meet you!

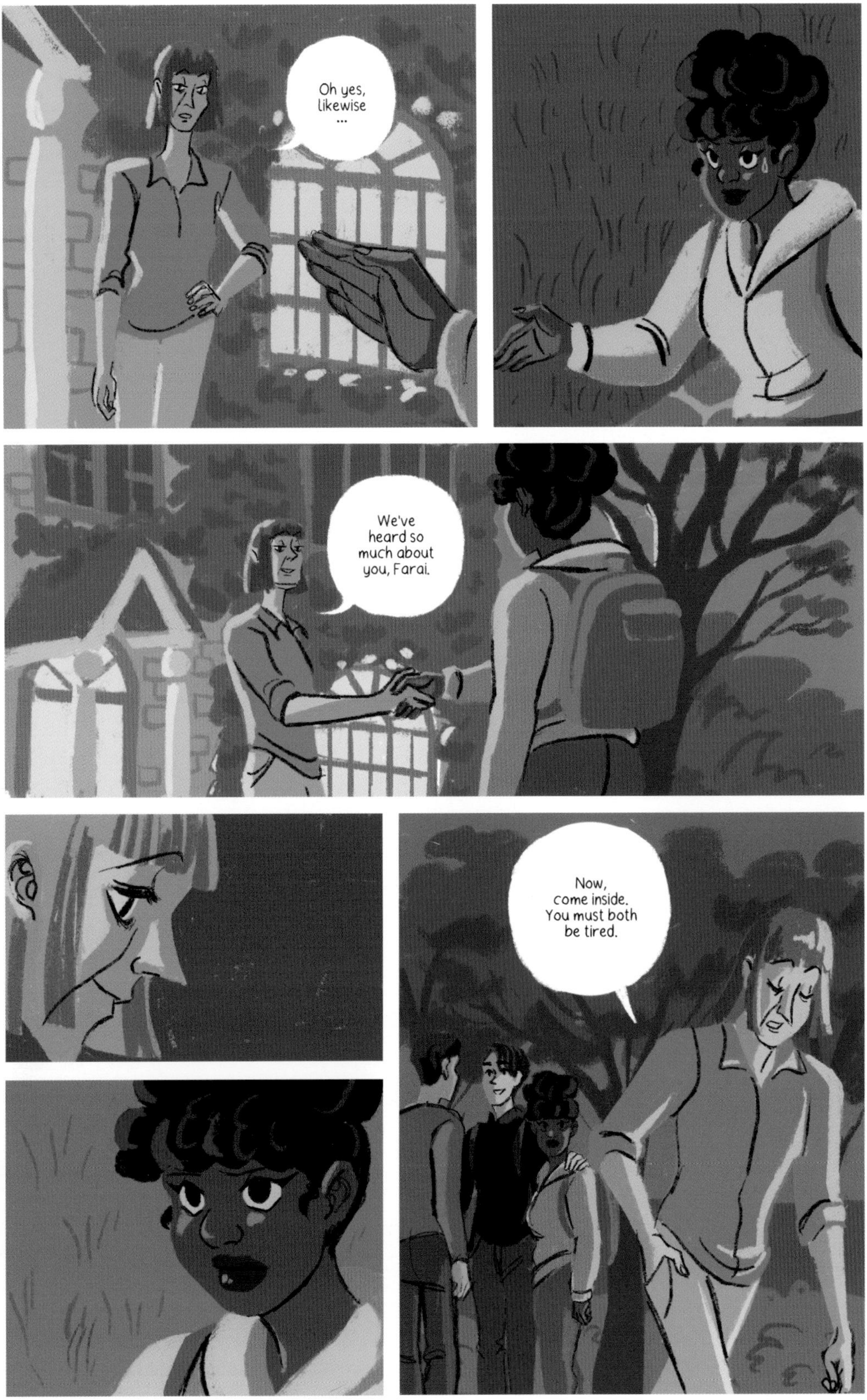
Oh yes, likewise ...
We've heard so much about you, Farai.
Now, come inside. You must both be tired.

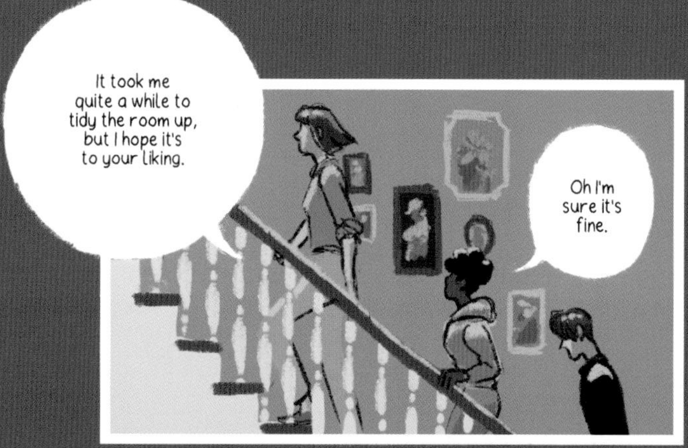
It took me quite a while to tidy the room up, but I hope it's to your liking.
Oh I'm sure it's fine.

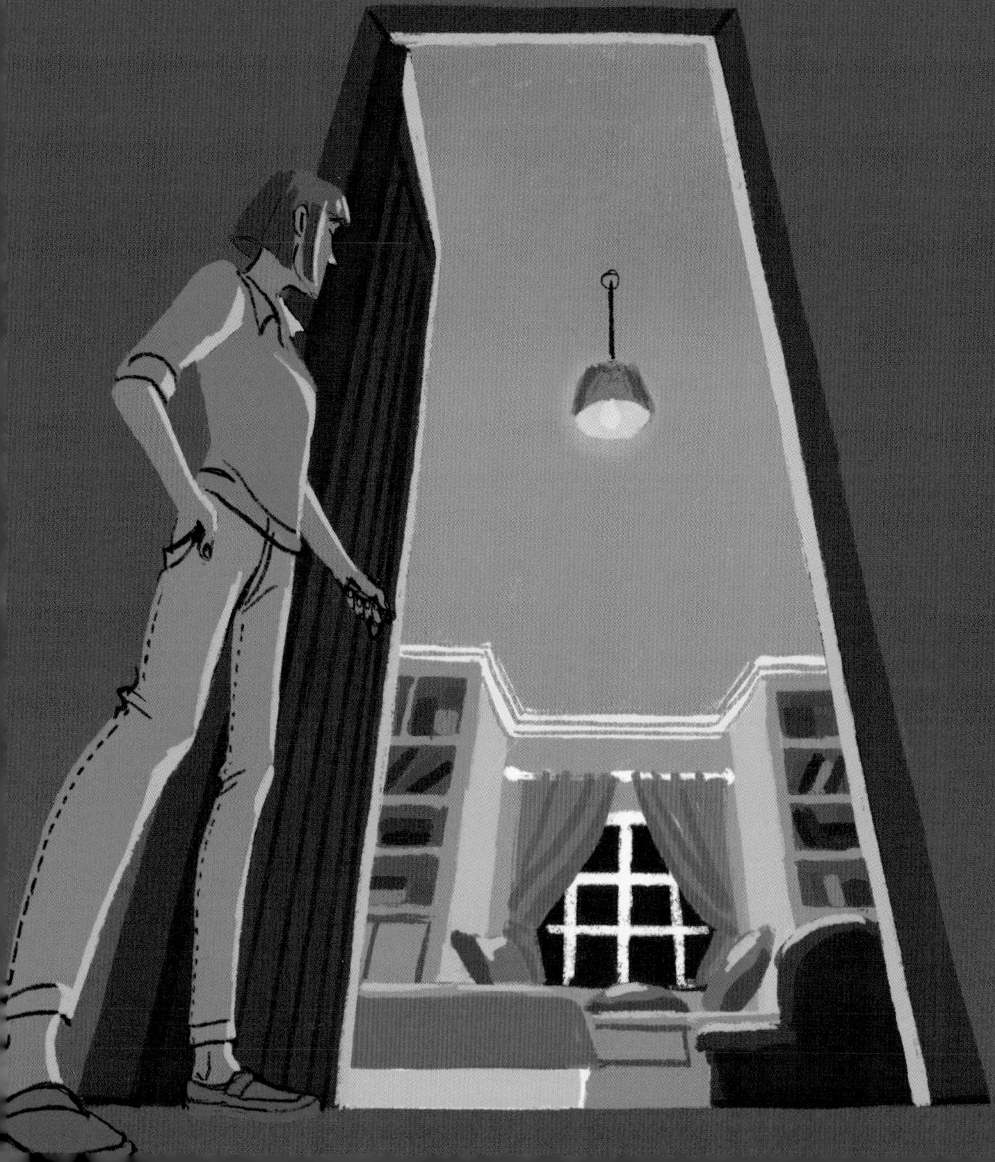

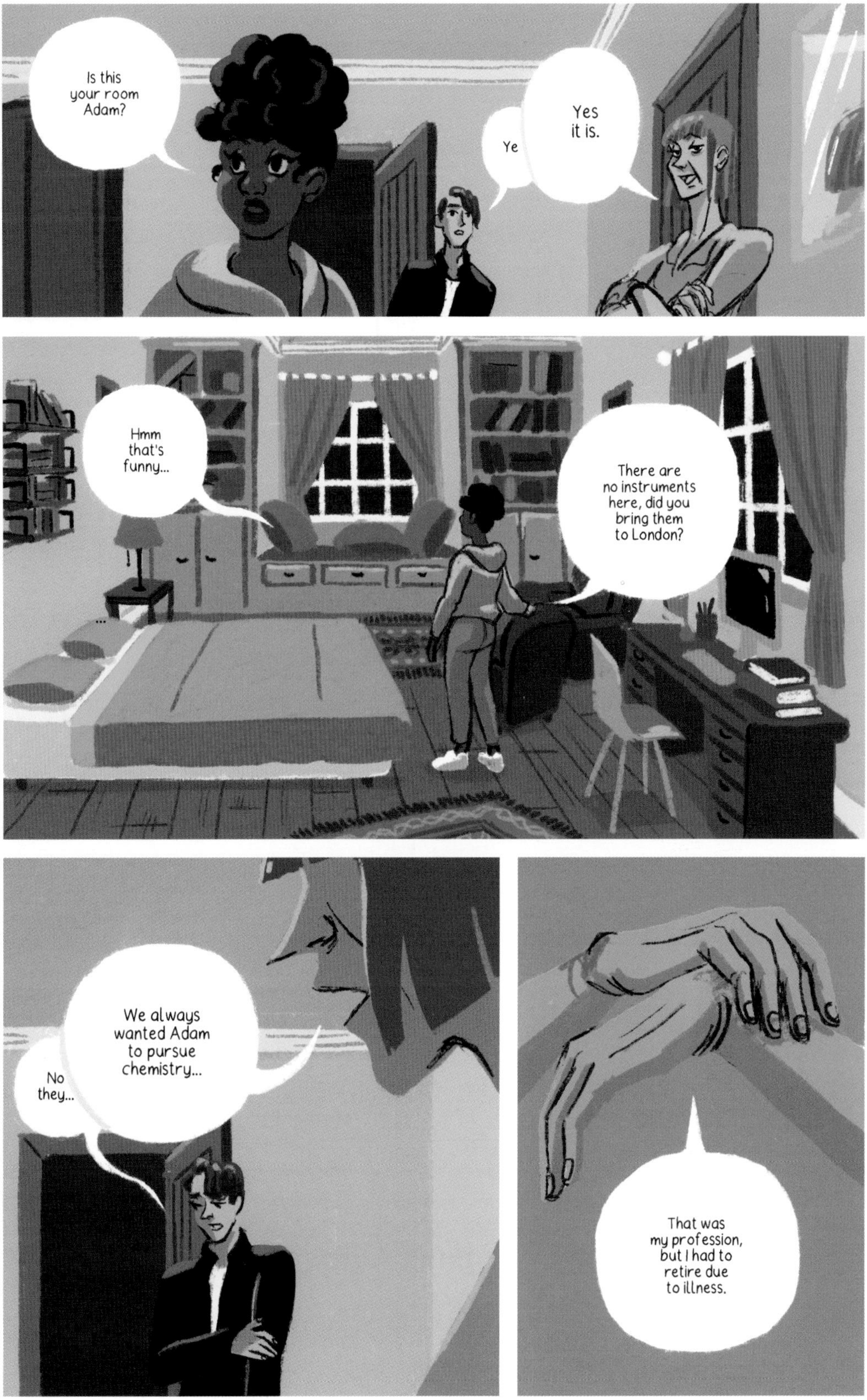
Is this your room Adam?
Ye
Yes it is.
Hmm that's funny...
There are no instruments here, did you bring them to London?
No they...
We always wanted Adam to pursue chemistry...
That was my profession, but I had to retire due to illness.

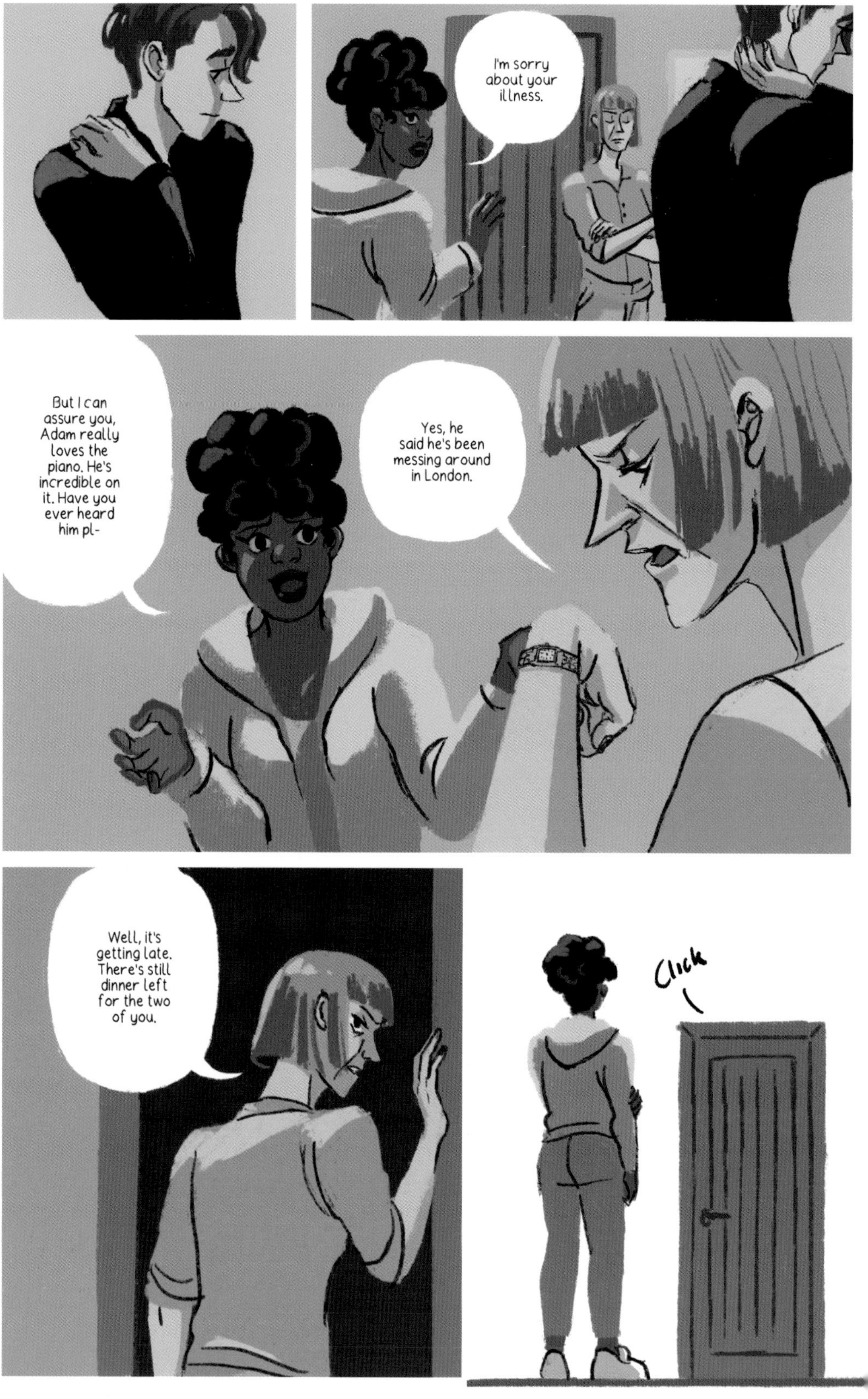
I'm sorry about your illness.
But I can assure you, Adam really loves the piano. He's incredible on it. Have you ever heard him pl-
Yes, he said he's been messing around in London.
Well, it's getting late. There's still dinner left for the two of you.
Click

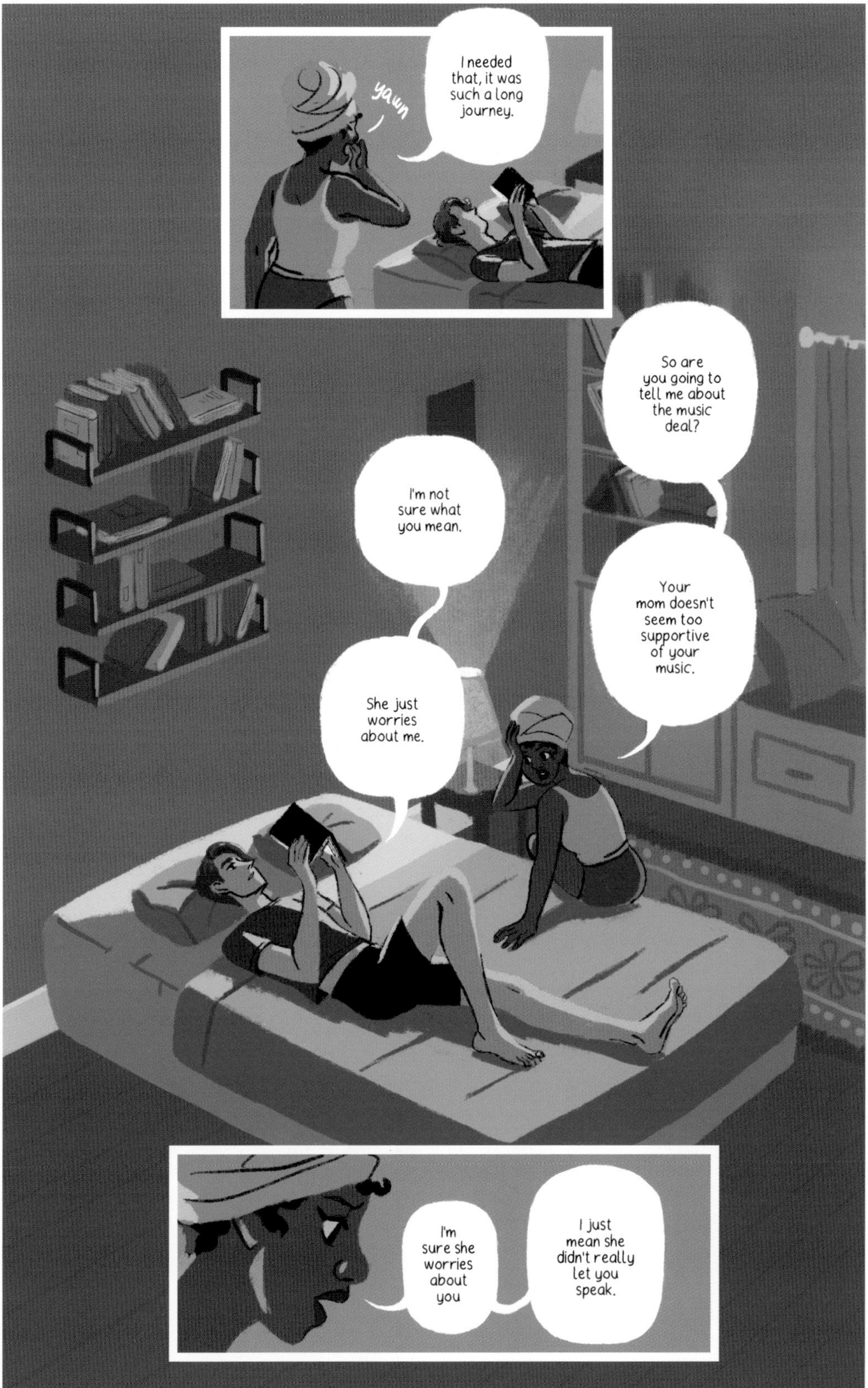
yawn
I needed that, it was such a long journey.
So are you going to tell me about the music deal?
Your mom doesn't seem too supportive of your music.
I'm not sure what you mean.
She just worries about me.
I just mean she didn't really let you speak.
I'm sure she worries about you

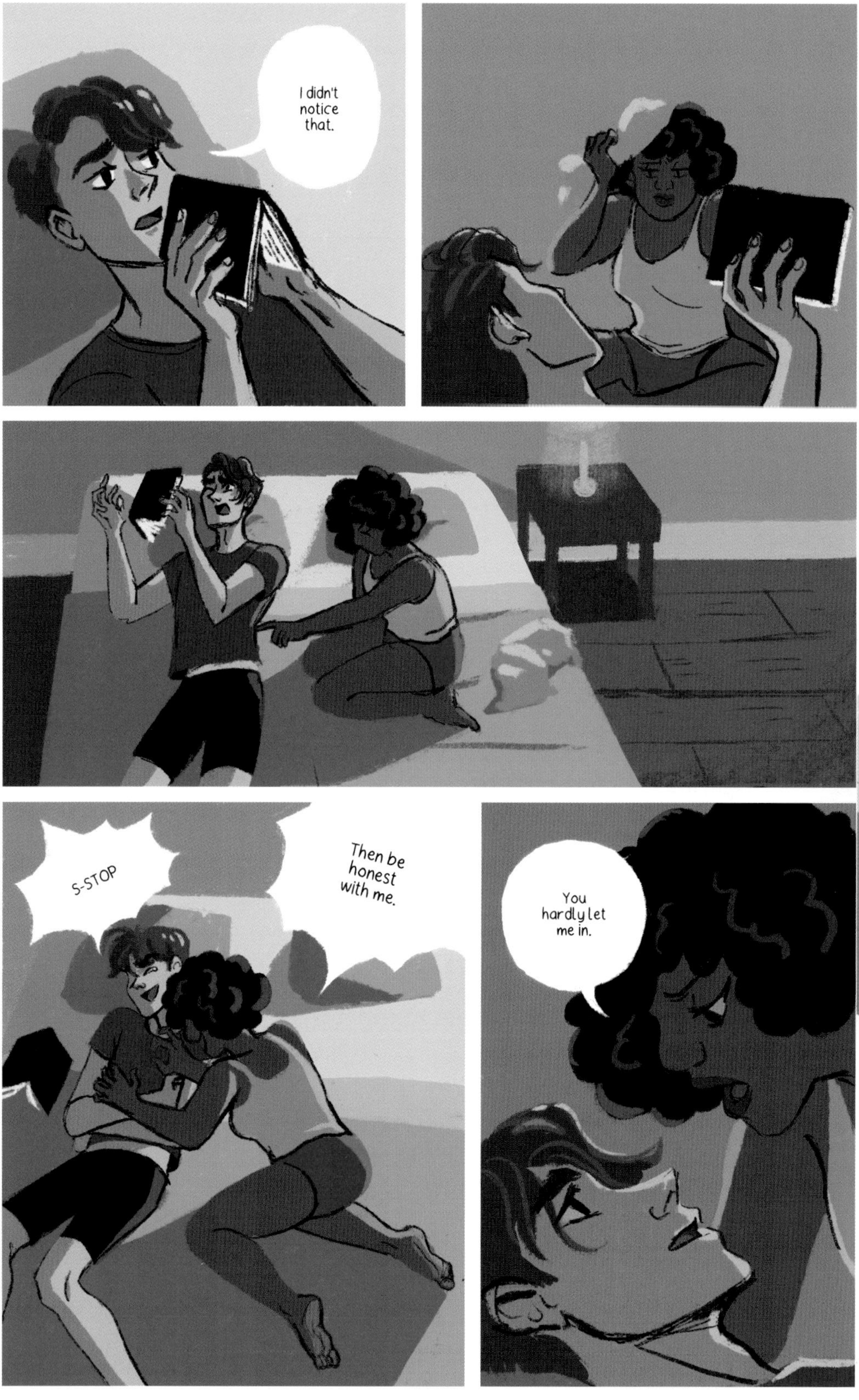
I didn't notice that.
S-STOP
Then be honest with me.
You hardly let me in.

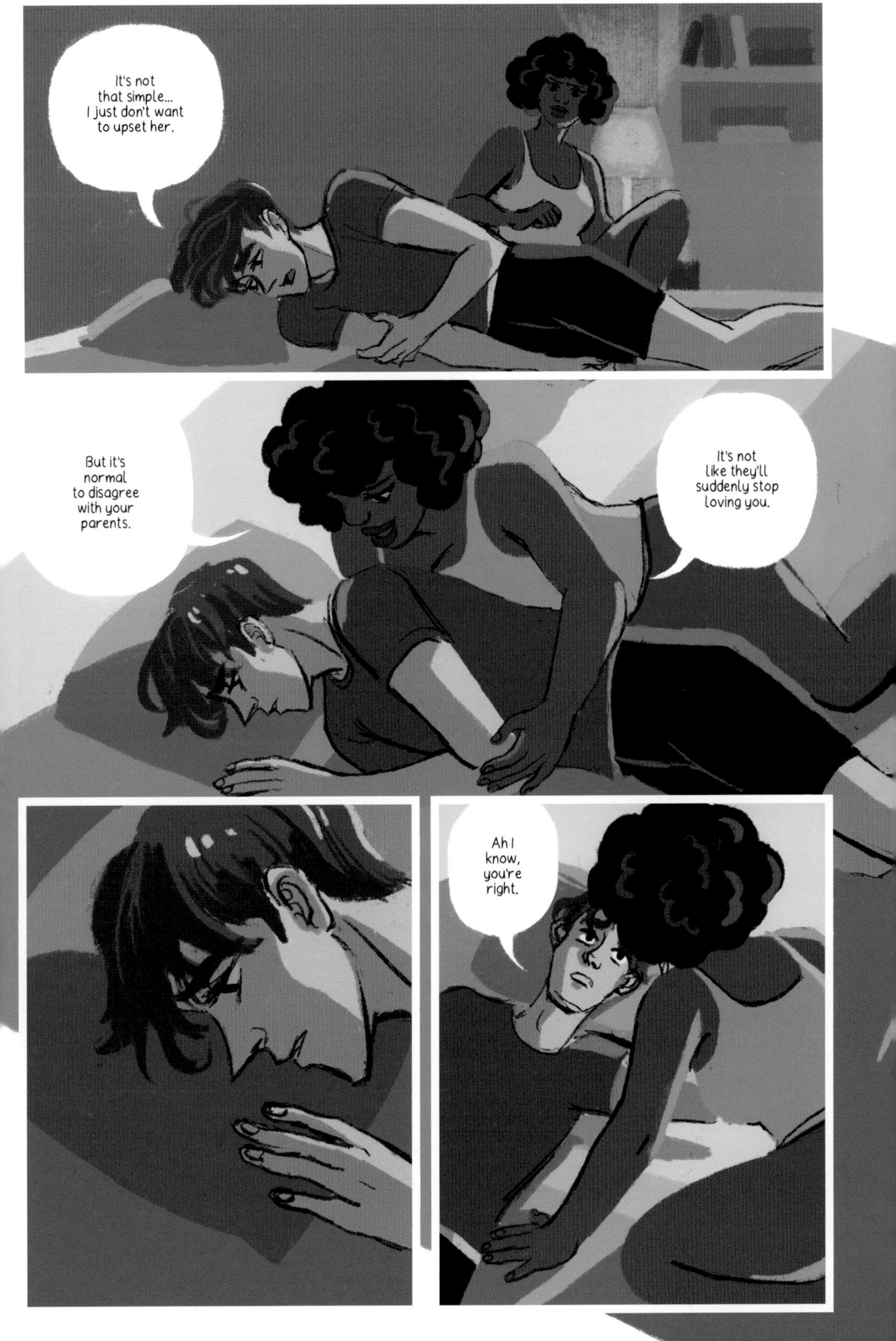
It's not that simple... I just don't want to upset her.
But it's normal to disagree with your parents.
It's not like they'll suddenly stop loving you.
Ah I know, you're right.

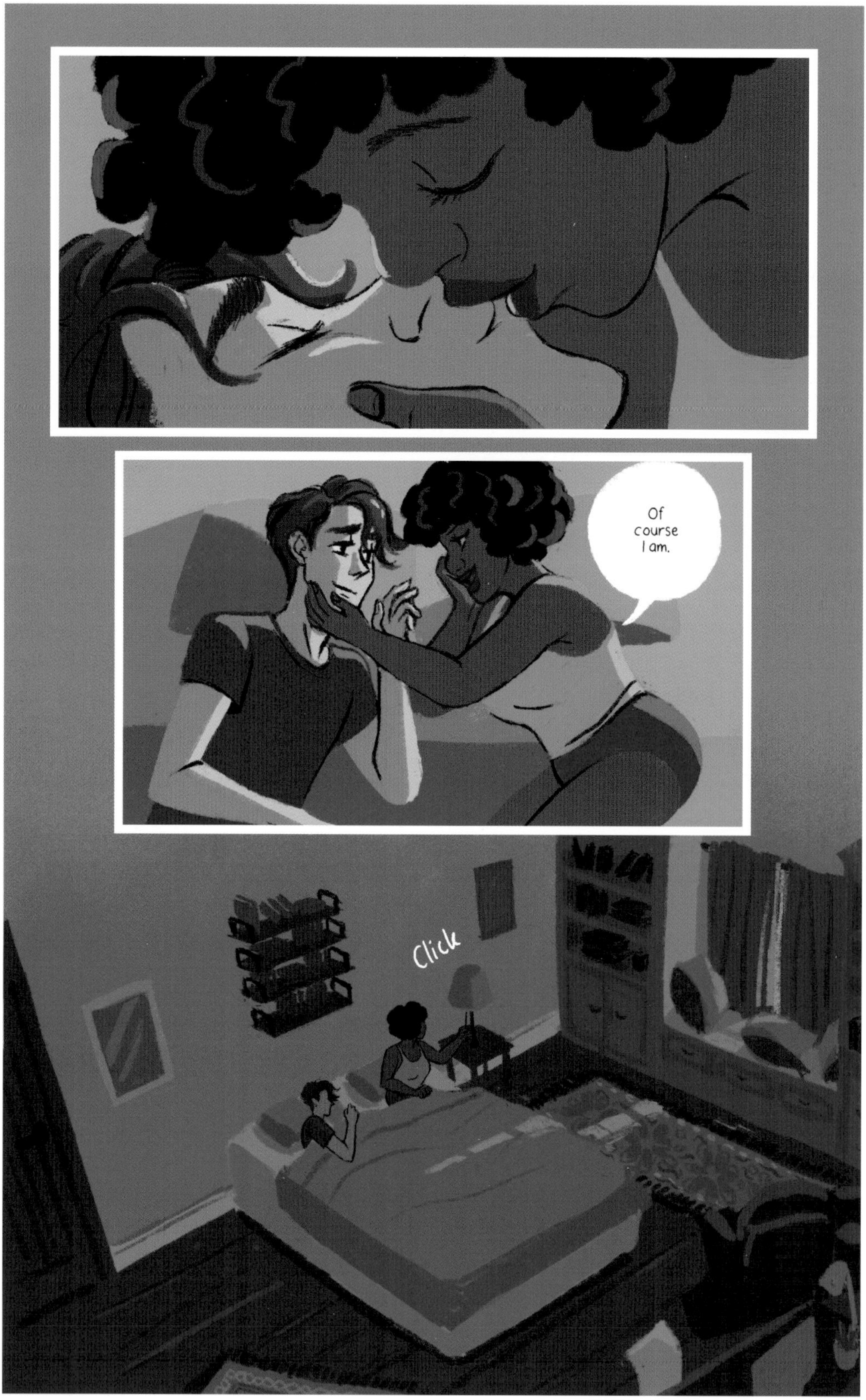
Of course I am.
Click

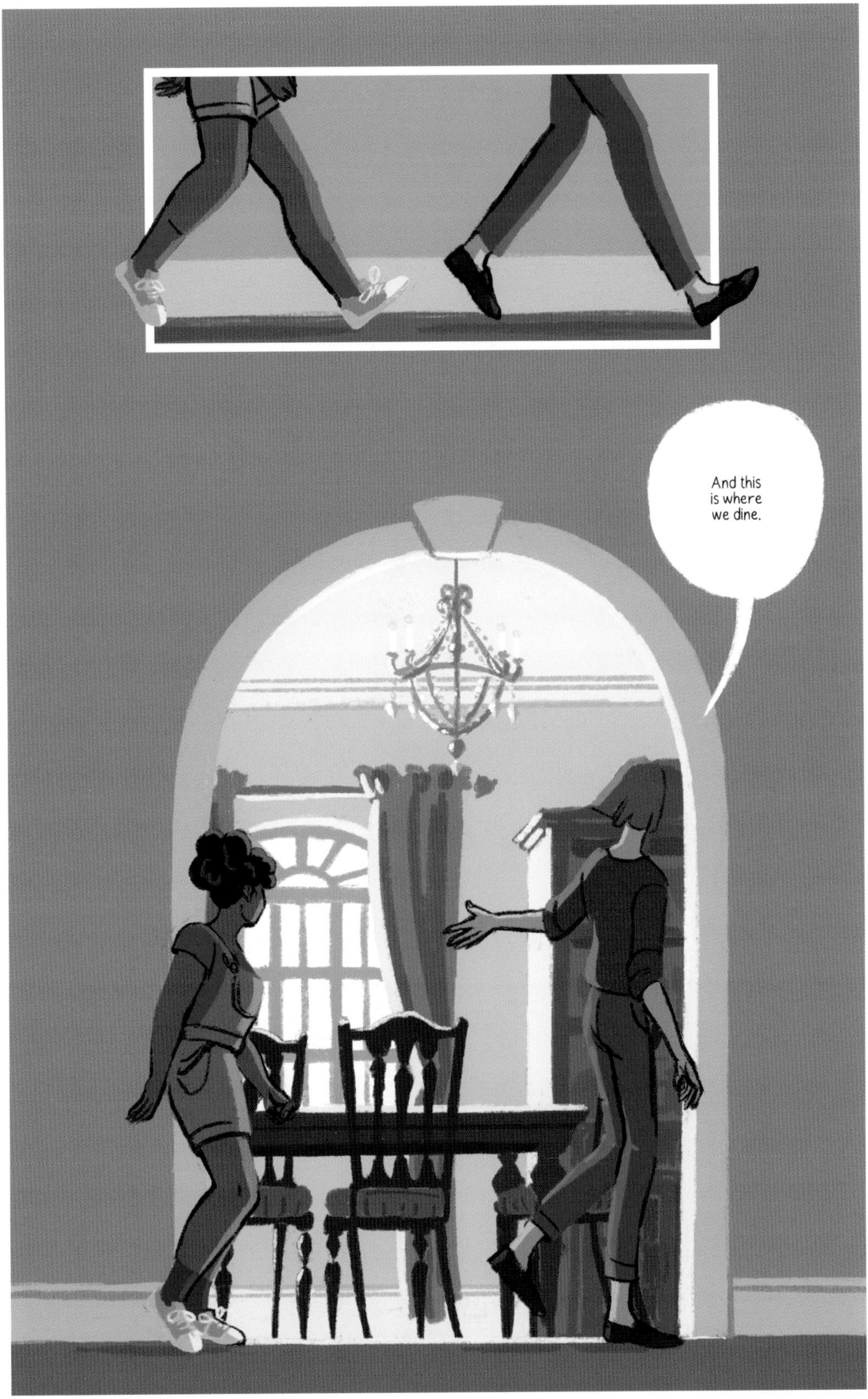
And this is where we dine.

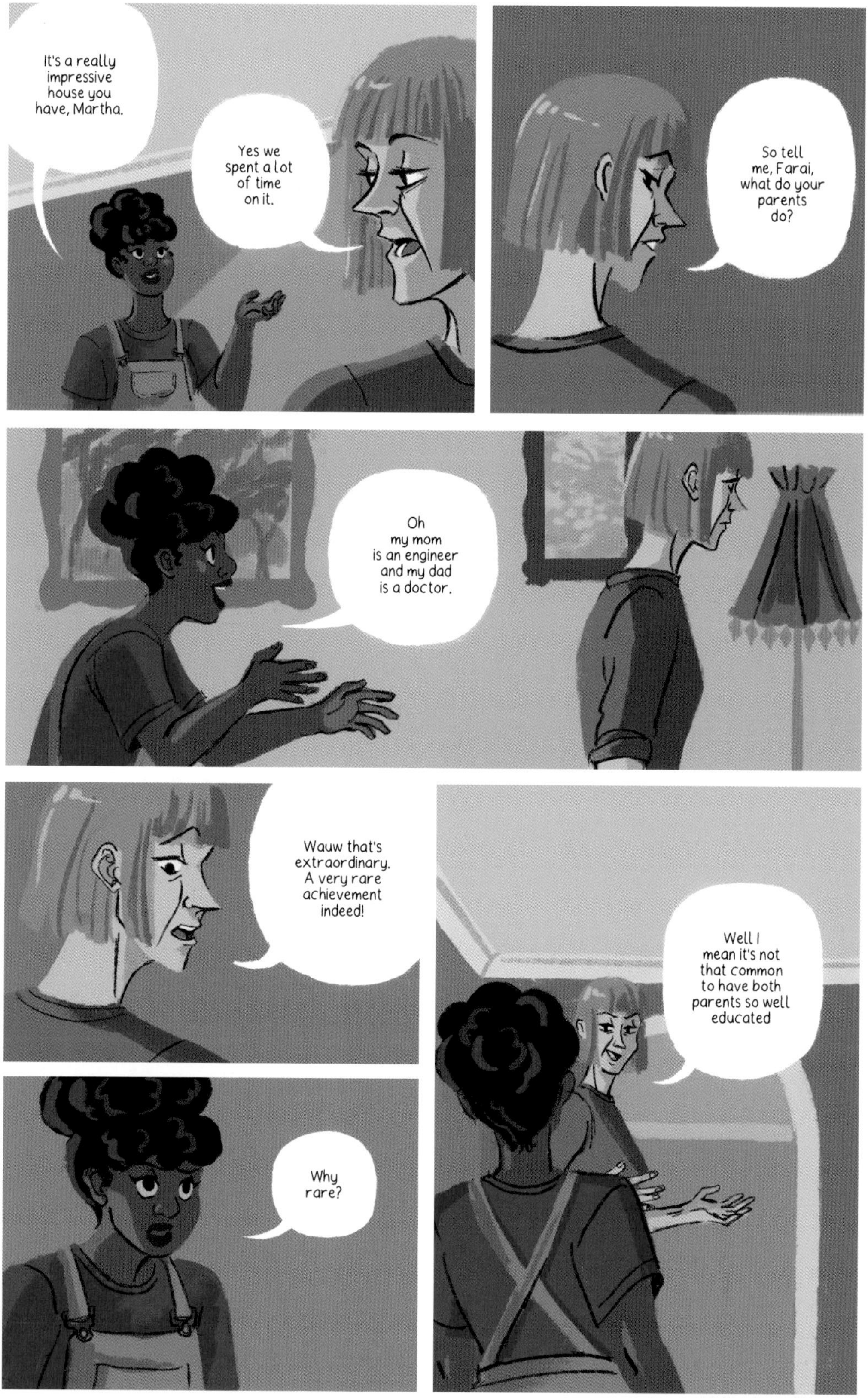

It's a really impressive house you have, Martha.
Yes we spent a lot of time on it.
So tell me, Farai, what do your parents do?
Oh my mom is an engineer and my dad is a doctor.
Wauw that's extraordinary. A very rare achievement indeed!
Why rare?
Well I mean it's not that common to have both parents so well educated

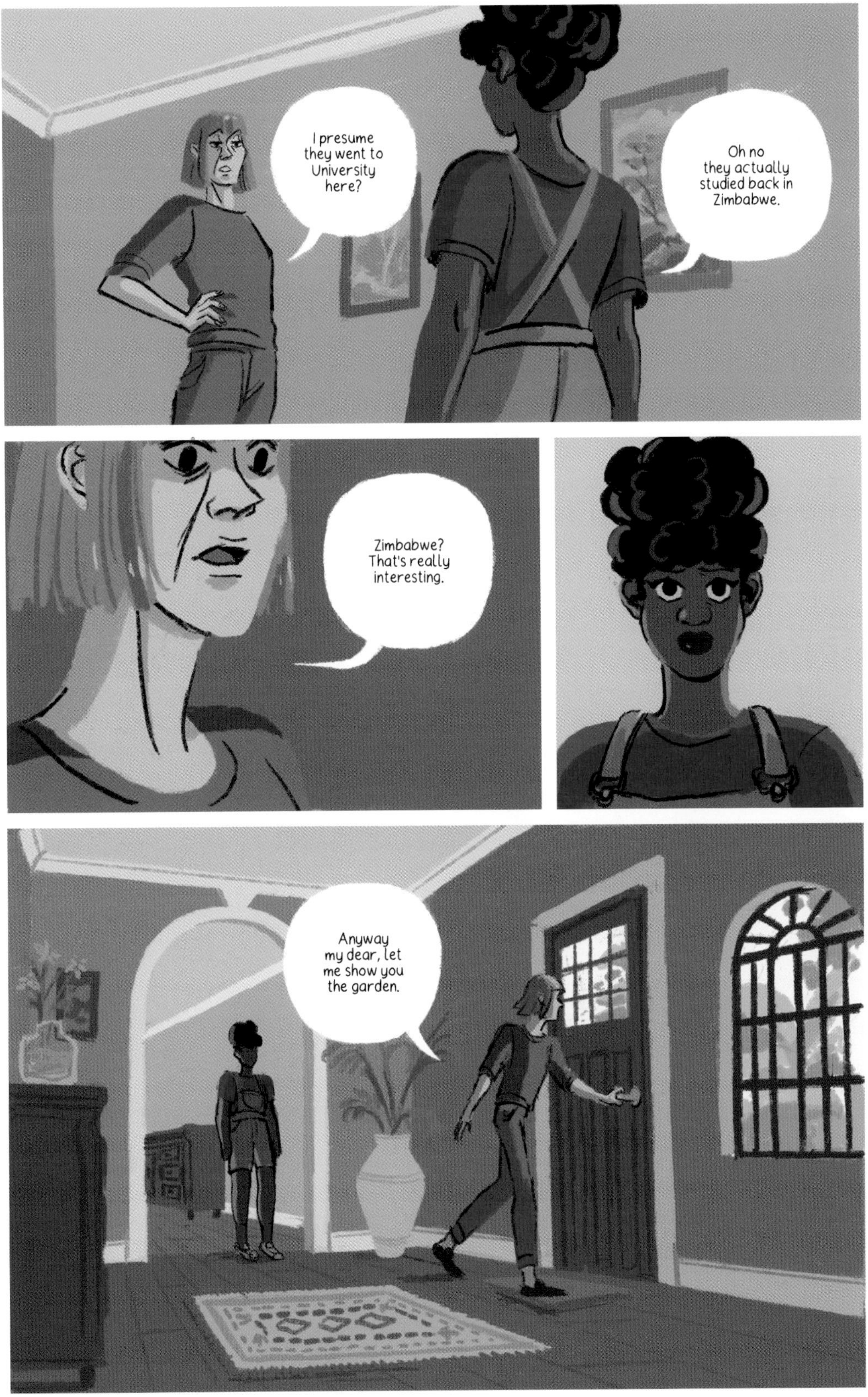
I presume they went to University here?
Oh no they actually studied back in Zimbabwe.
Zimbabwe? That's really interesting.
Anyway my dear, let me show you the garden.

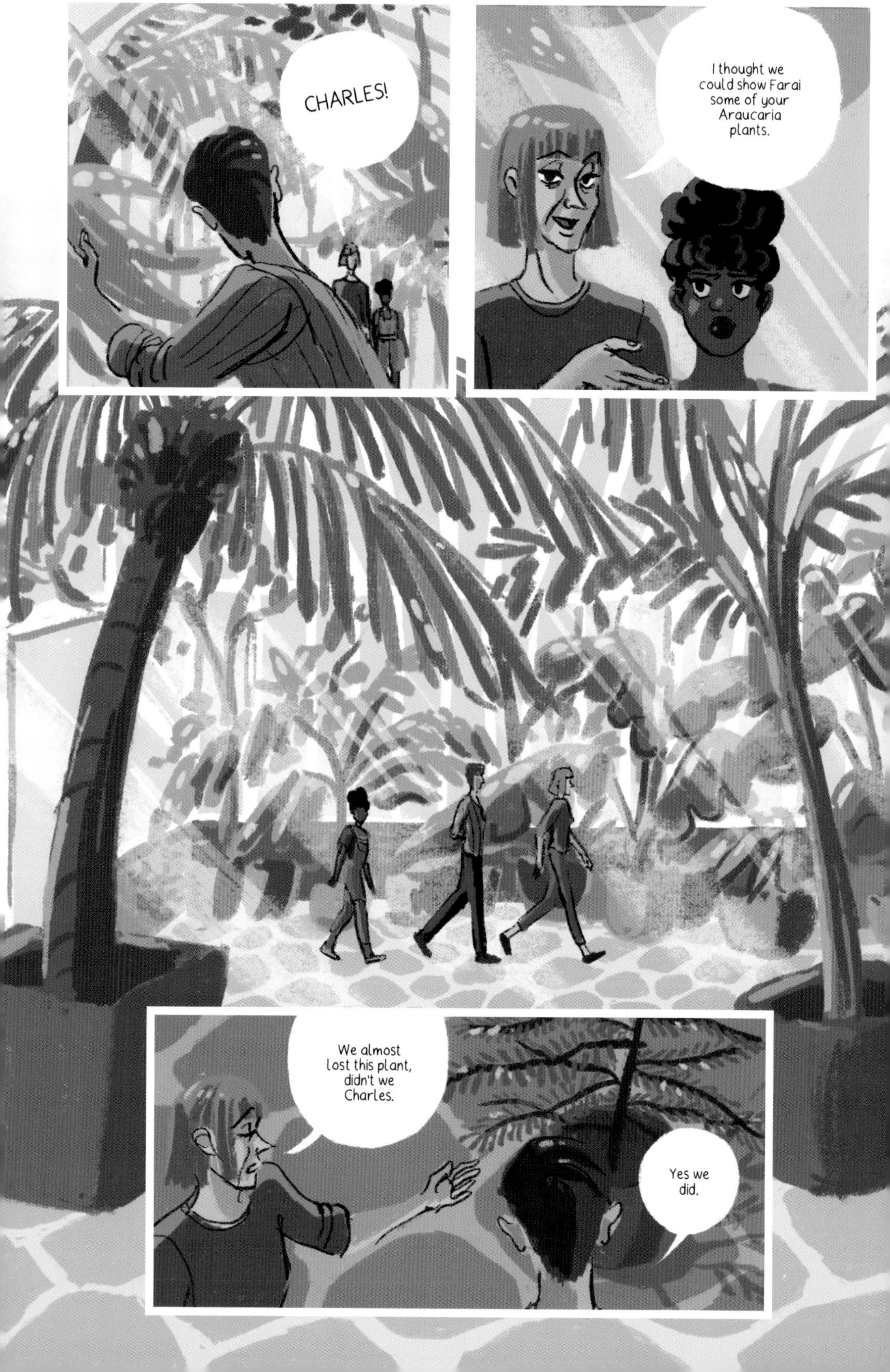
CHARLES!
I thought we could show Farai some of your Araucaria plants.
We almost lost this plant, didn't we Charles.
Yes we did.

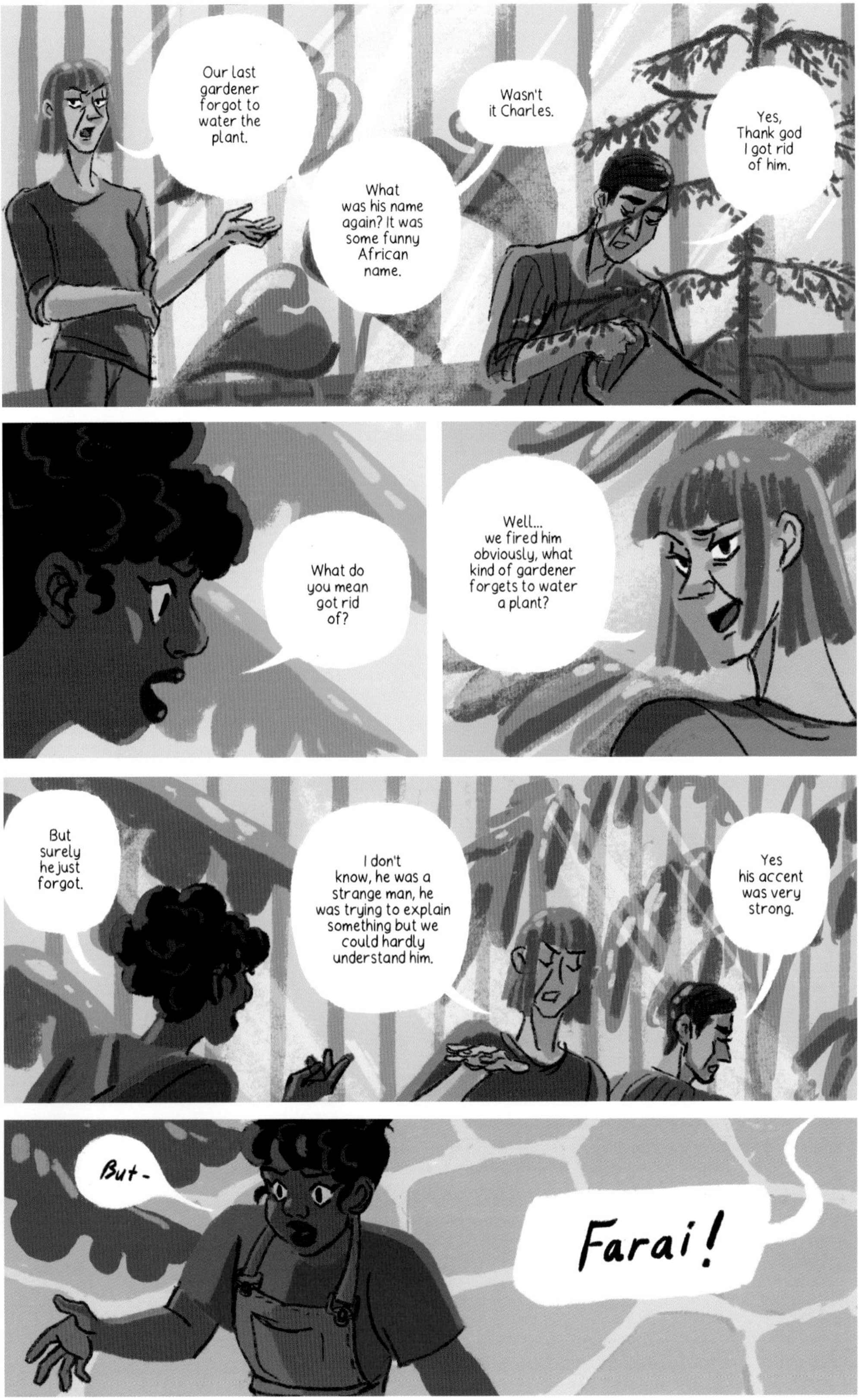
Our last gardener forgot to water the plant.
What was his name again? It was some funny African name.
Wasn't it Charles.
Yes, Thank god I got rid of him.
What do you mean got rid of?
Well... we fired him obviously, what kind of gardener forgets to water a plant?
But surely he just forgot.
I don't know, he was a strange man, he was trying to explain something but we could hardly understand him.
Yes his accent was very strong.
But-
Farai!

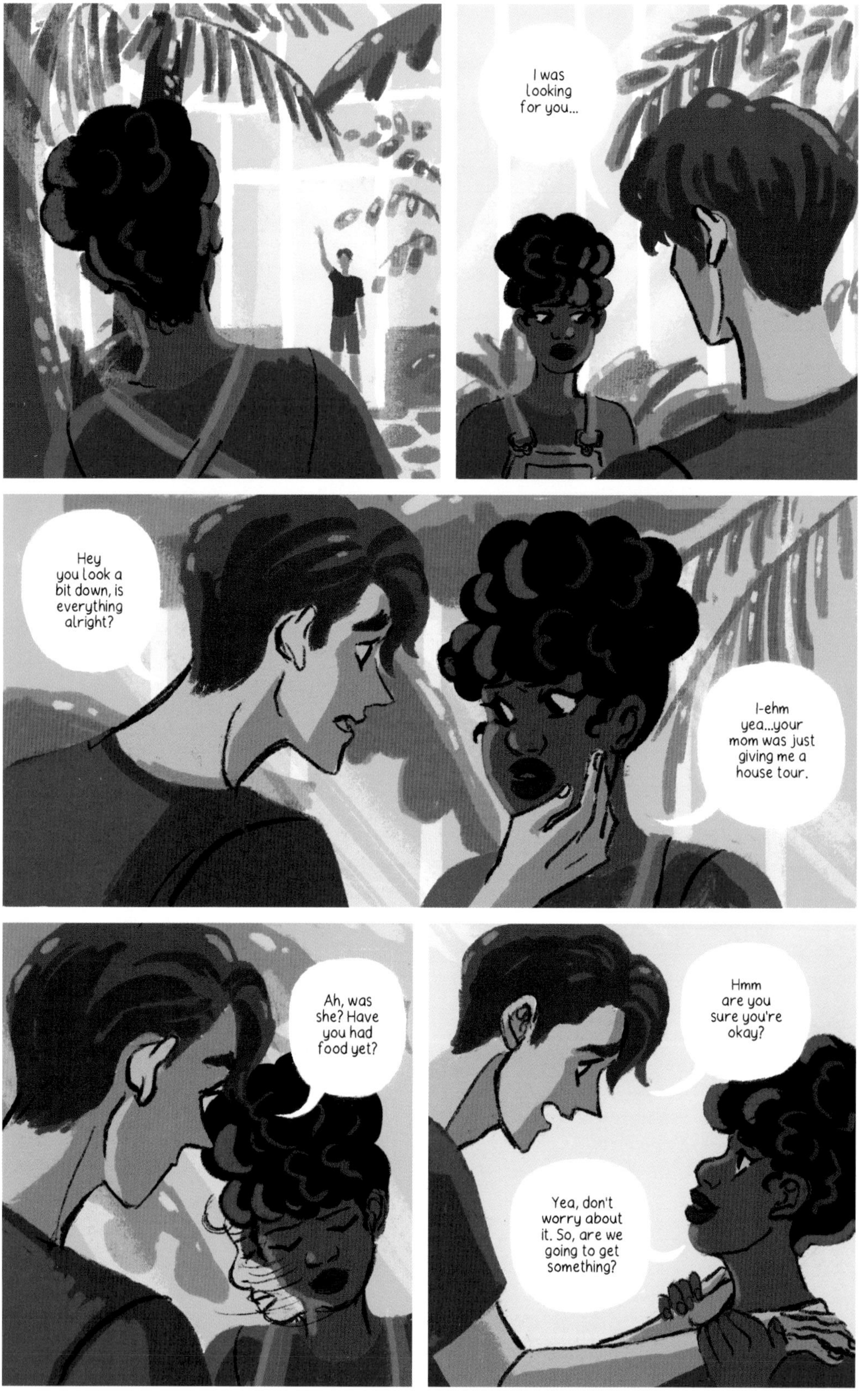
I was looking for you...
Hey you look a bit down, is everything alright?
I-ehm yea...your mom was just giving me a house tour.
Ah, was she? Have you had food yet?
Hmm are you sure you're okay?
Yea, don't worry about it. So, are we going to get something?

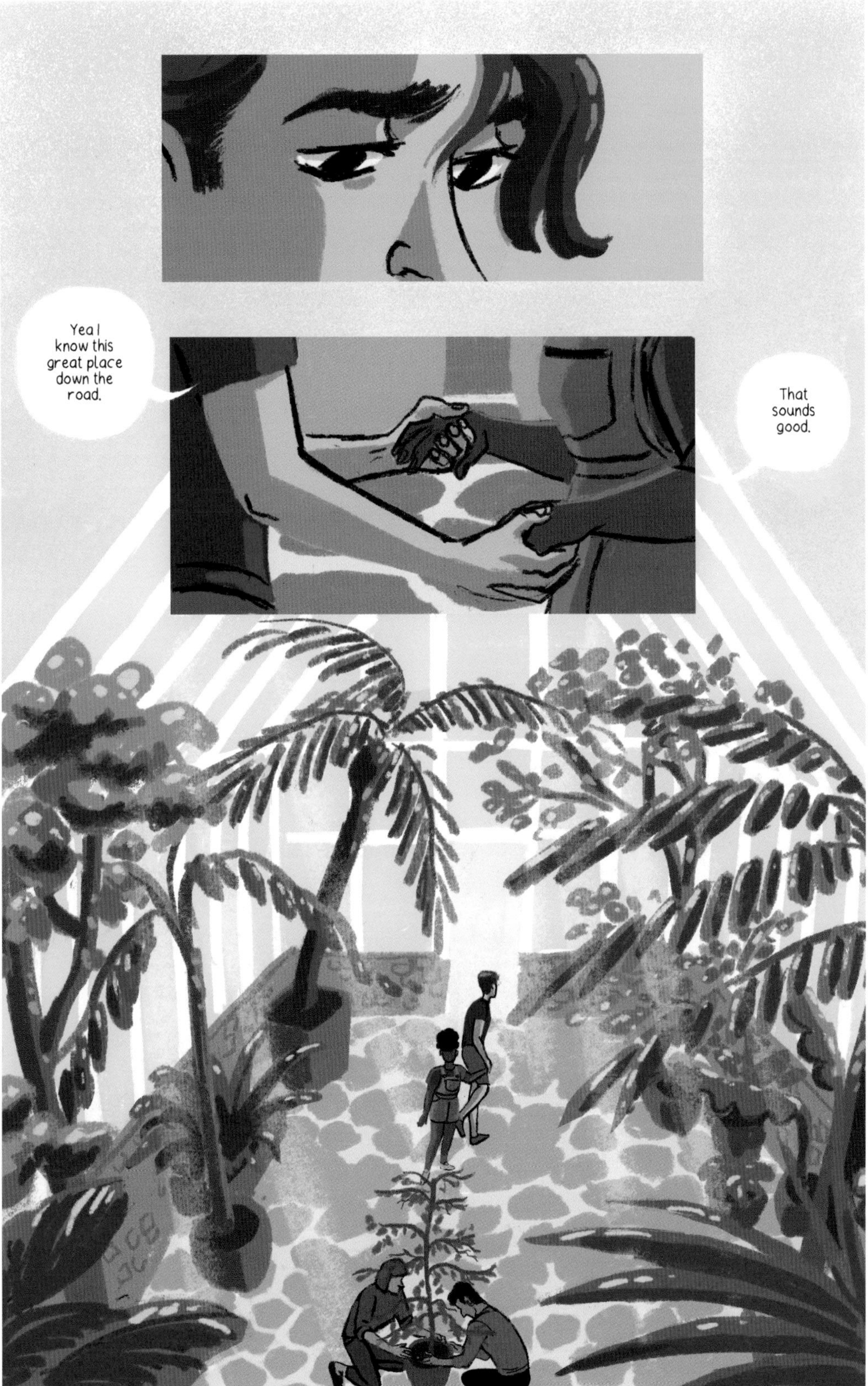
Yea I know this great place down the road.
That sounds good.

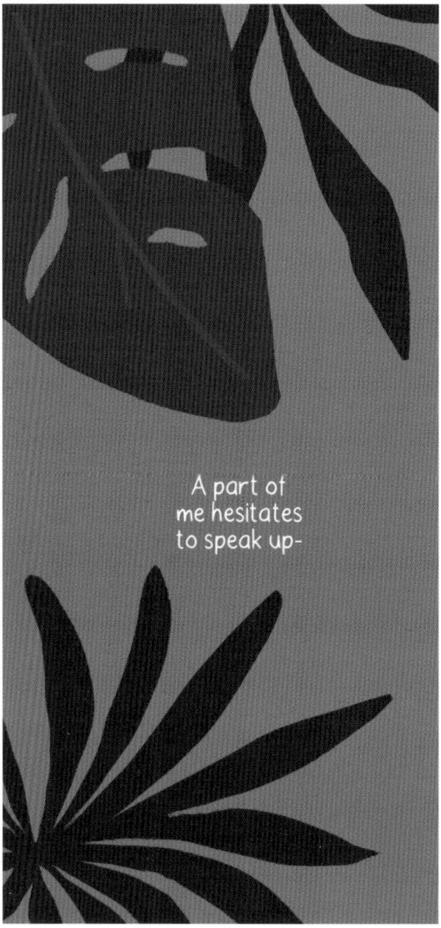
A part of
me hesitates
to speak up-

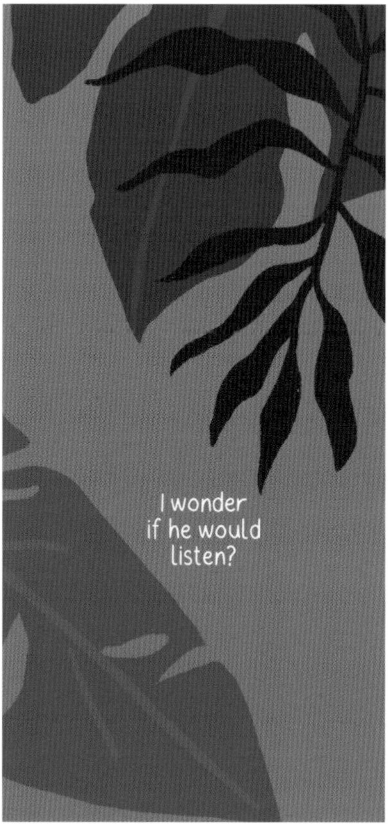
I wonder
if he would
listen?

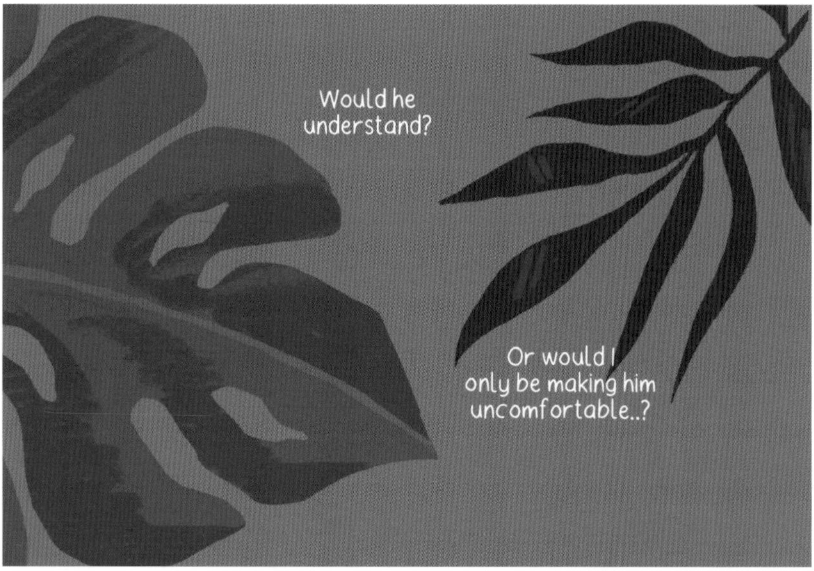
Would he
understand?
Or would I
only be making him
uncomfortable..?

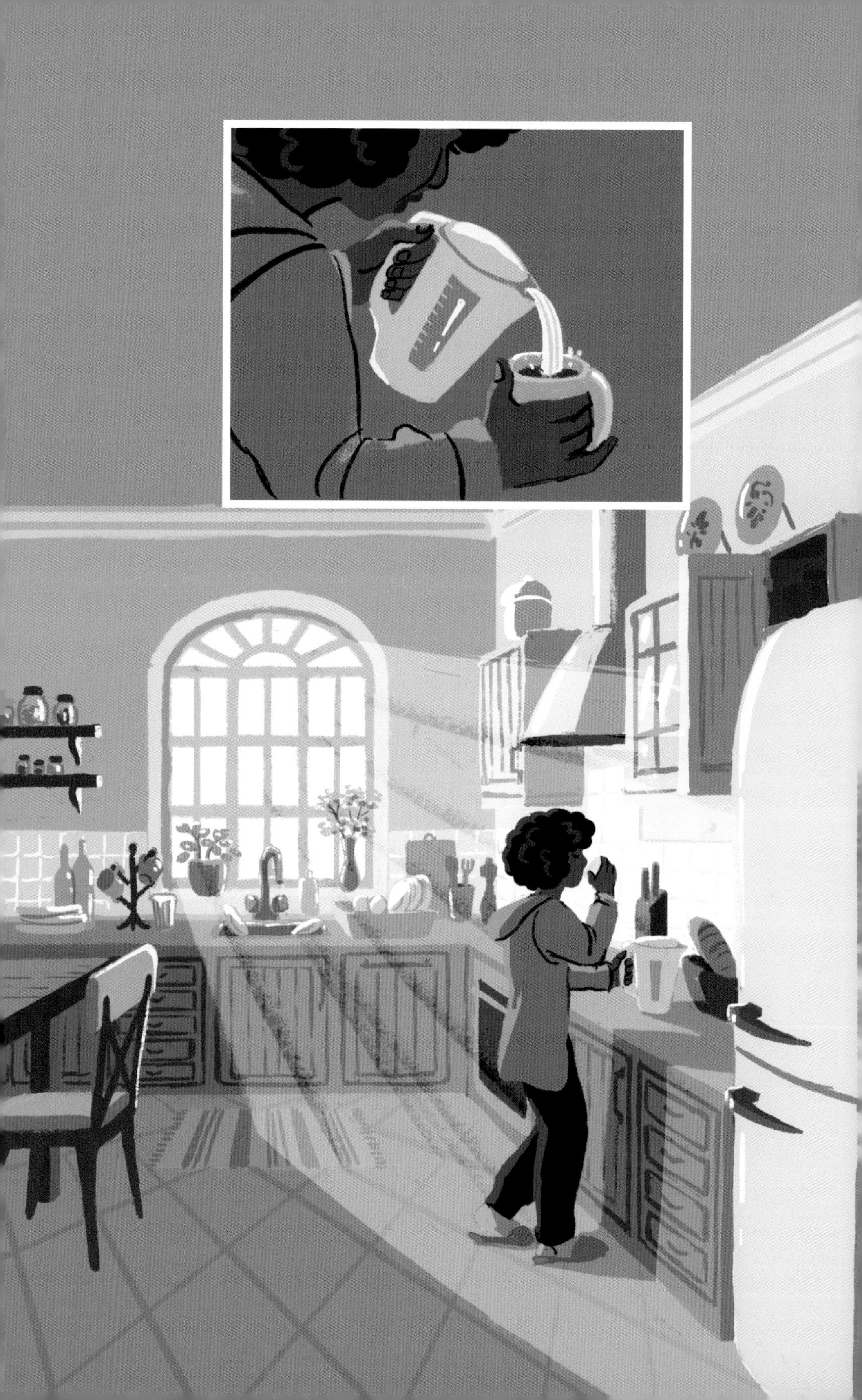

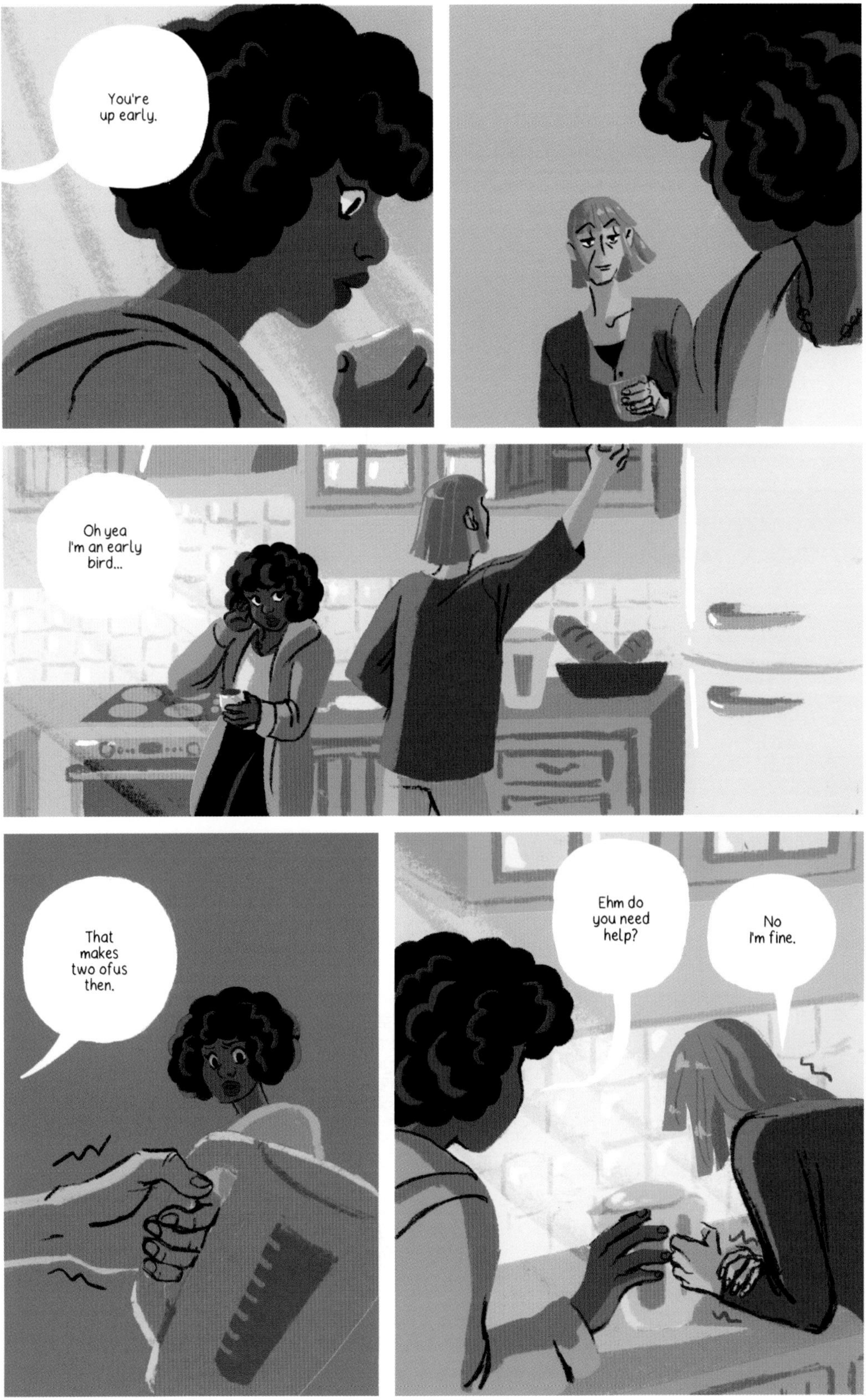
You're up early.
Oh yea I'm an early bird...
That makes two ofus then.
Ehm do you need help?
No I'm fine.

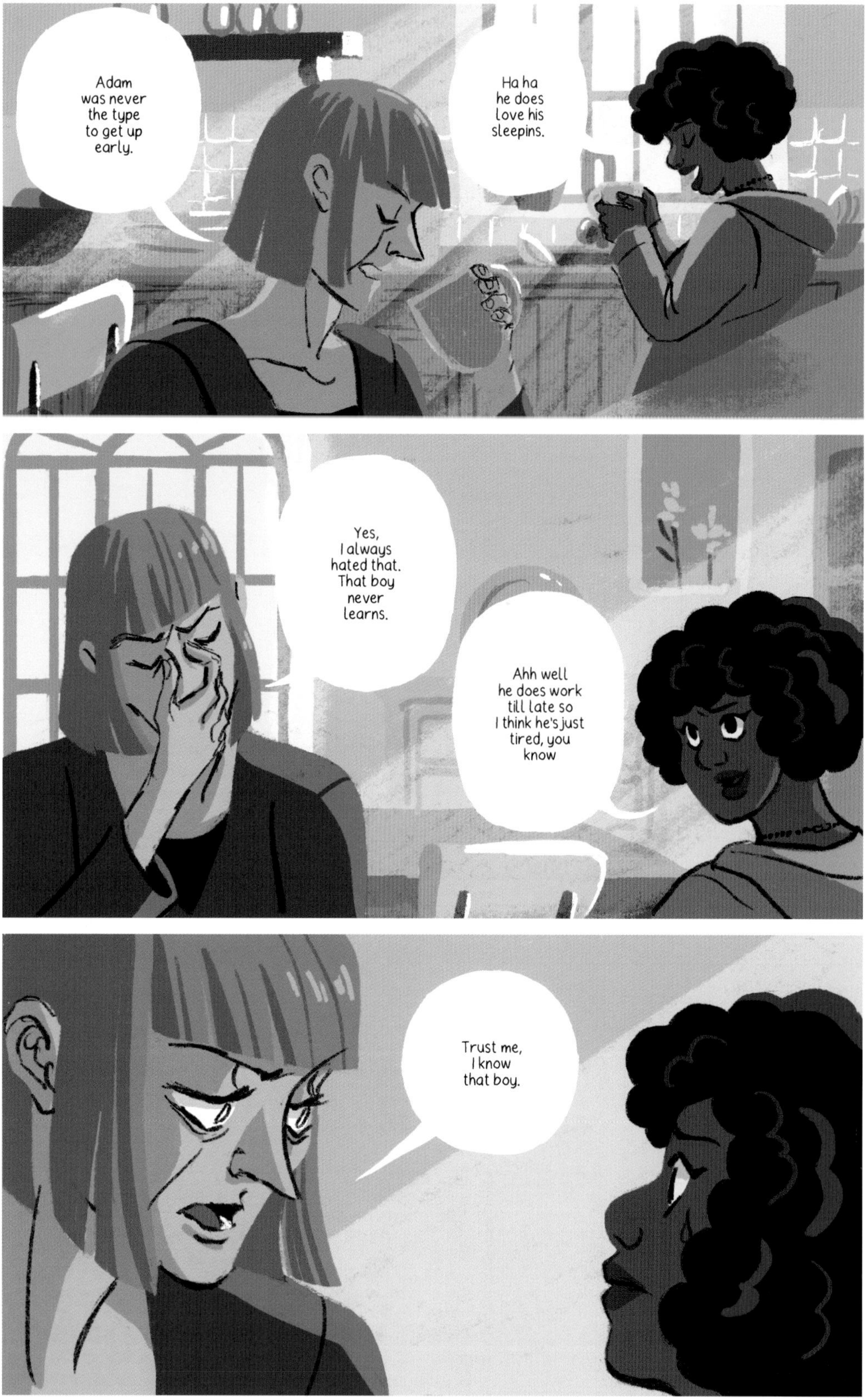
Adam was never the type to get up early.
Ha ha he does love his sleepins.
Yes, I always hated that. That boy never learns.
Ahh well he does work till late so I think he's just tired, you know
Trust me, I know that boy.

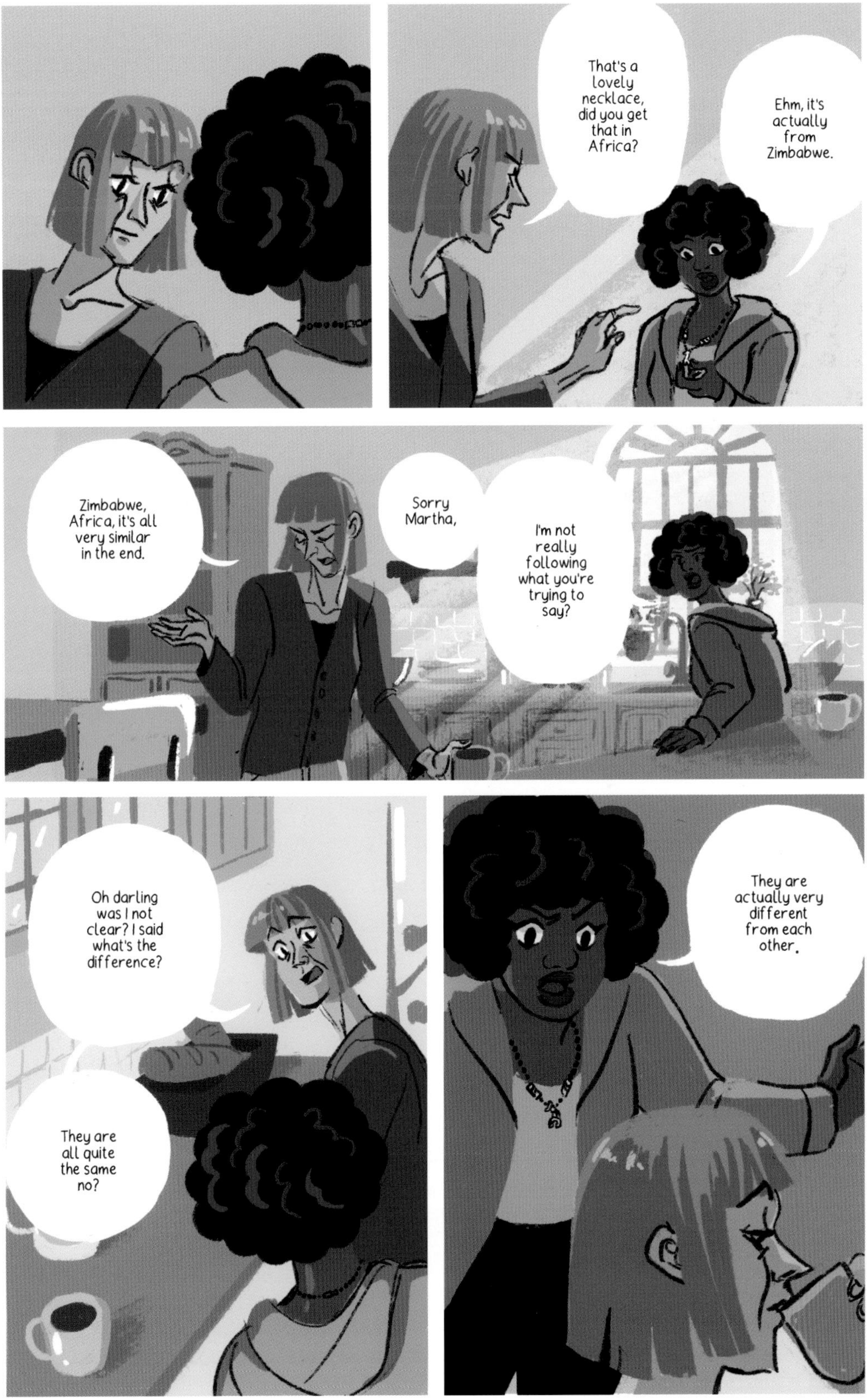
That's a lovely necklace, did you get that in Africa?
Ehm, it's actually from Zimbabwe.
Zimbabwe, Africa, it's all very similar in the end.
Sorry Martha,
I'm not really following what you're trying to say?
Oh darling was I not clear? I said what's the difference?
They are all quite the same no?
They are actually very different from each other.

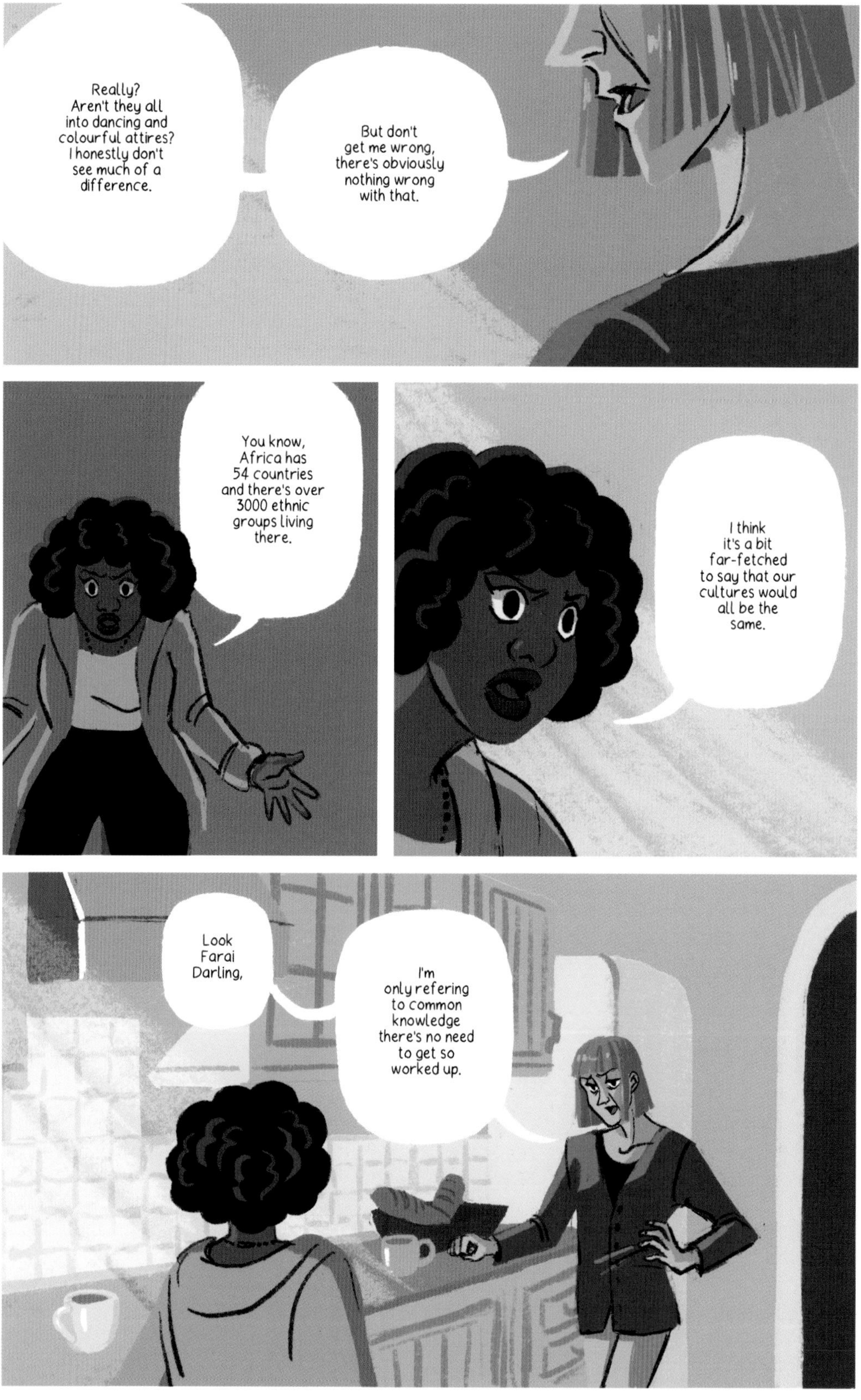
Really? Aren't they all into dancing and colourful attires? I honestly don't see much of a difference.
But don't get me wrong, there's obviously nothing wrong with that.
You know, Africa has 54 countries and there's over 3000 ethnic groups living there.
I think it's a bit far-fetched to say that our cultures would all be the same.
Look Farai Darling,
I'm only refering to common knowledge there's no need to get so worked up.

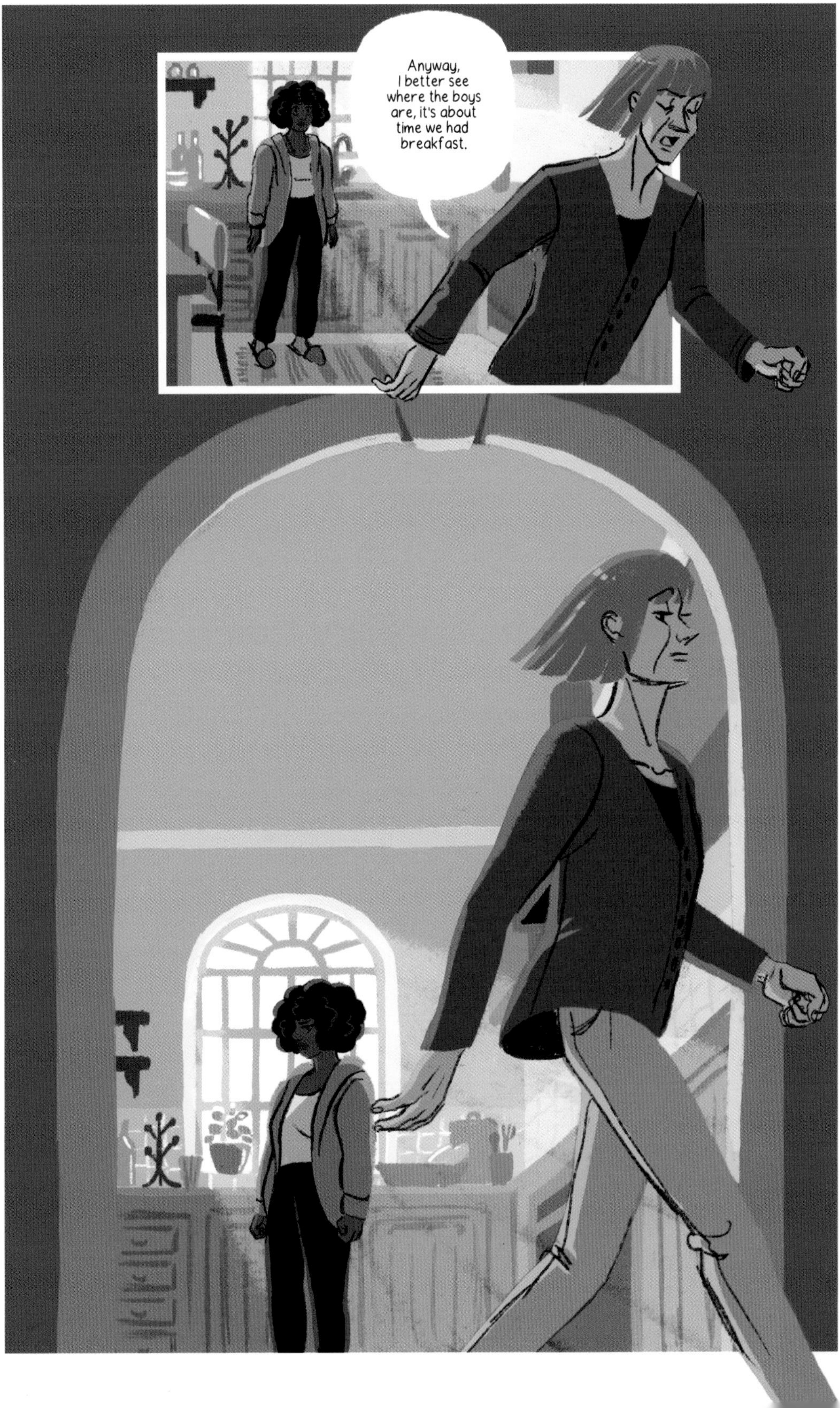
Anyway, I better see where the boys are, it's about time we had breakfast.

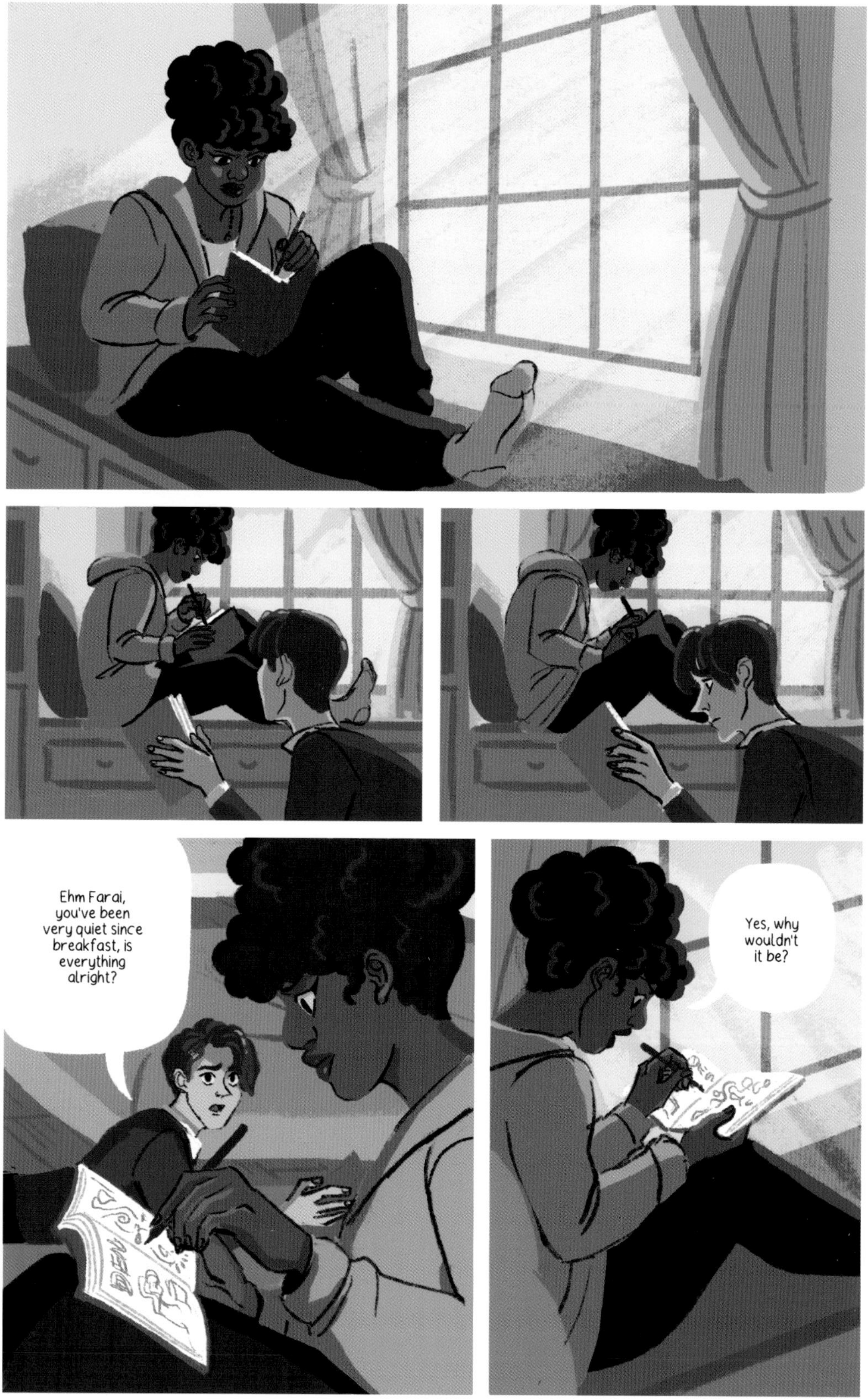
Ehm Farai, you've been very quiet since breakfast, is everything alright?
Yes, why wouldn't it be?

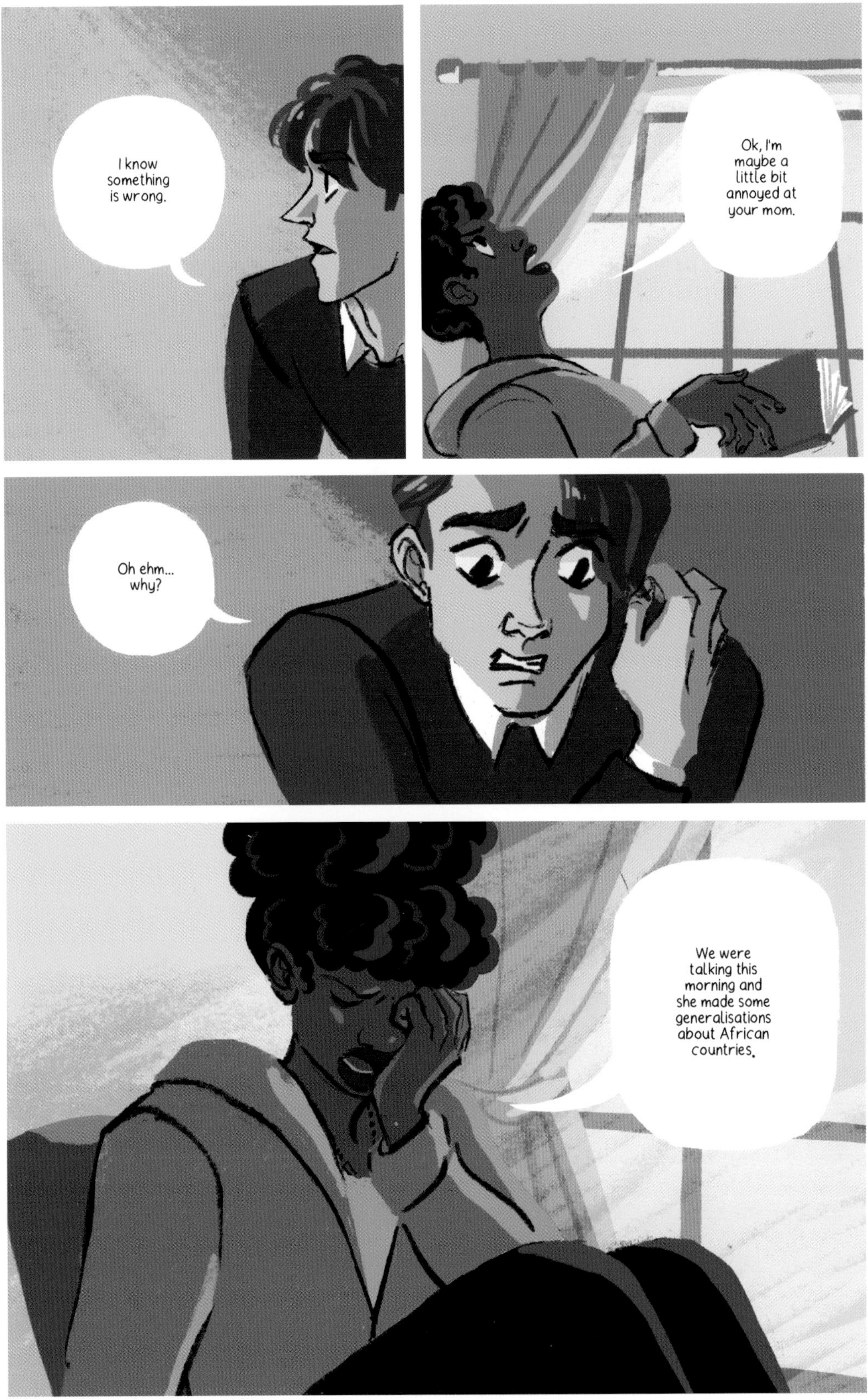
I know something is wrong.
Ok, I'm maybe a little bit annoyed at your mom.
Oh ehm... why?
We were talking this morning and she made some generalisations about African countries.

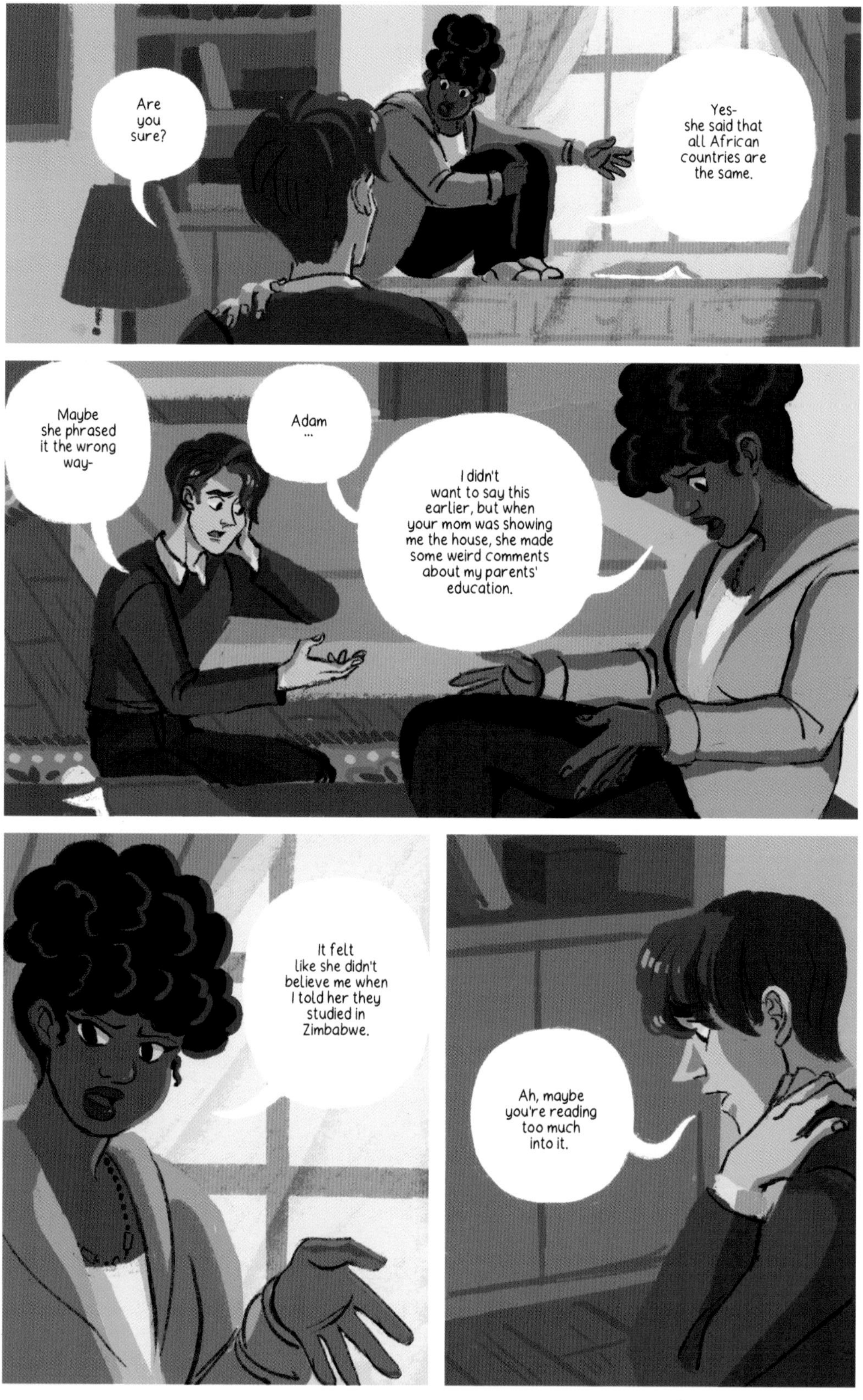
Are you sure?
Yes- she said that all African countries are the same.
Maybe she phrased it the wrong way-
Adam ...
I didn't want to say this earlier, but when your mom was showing me the house, she made some weird comments about my parents' education.
It felt like she didn't believe me when I told her they studied in Zimbabwe.
Ah, maybe you're reading too much into it.

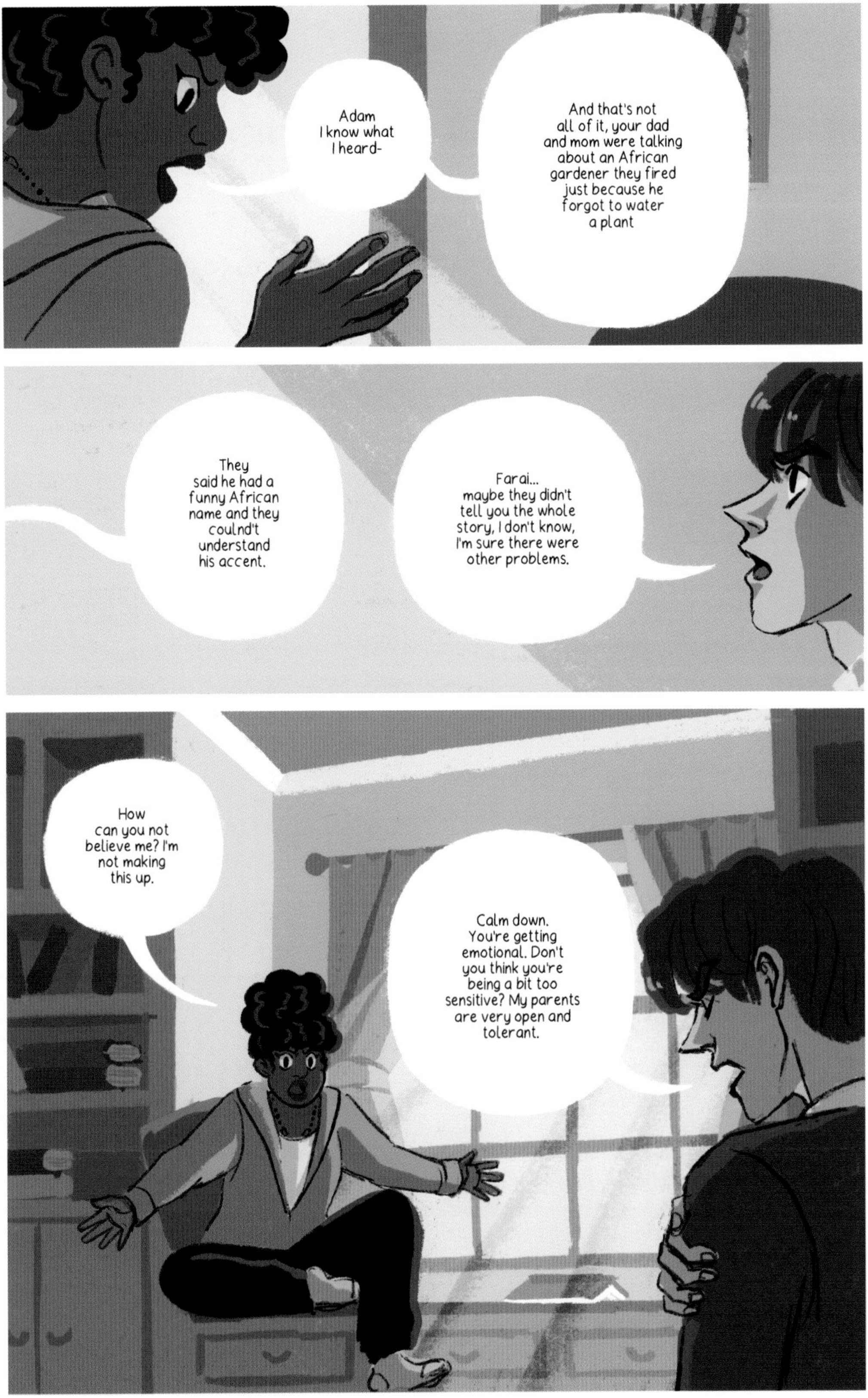
Adam I know what I heard-
And that's not all of it, your dad and mom were talking about an African gardener they fired just because he forgot to water a plant
They said he had a funny African name and they coulnd't understand his accent.
Farai... maybe they didn't tell you the whole story, I don't know, I'm sure there were other problems.
How can you not believe me? I'm not making this up.
Calm down. You're getting emotional. Don't you think you're being a bit too sensitive? My parents are very open and tolerant.

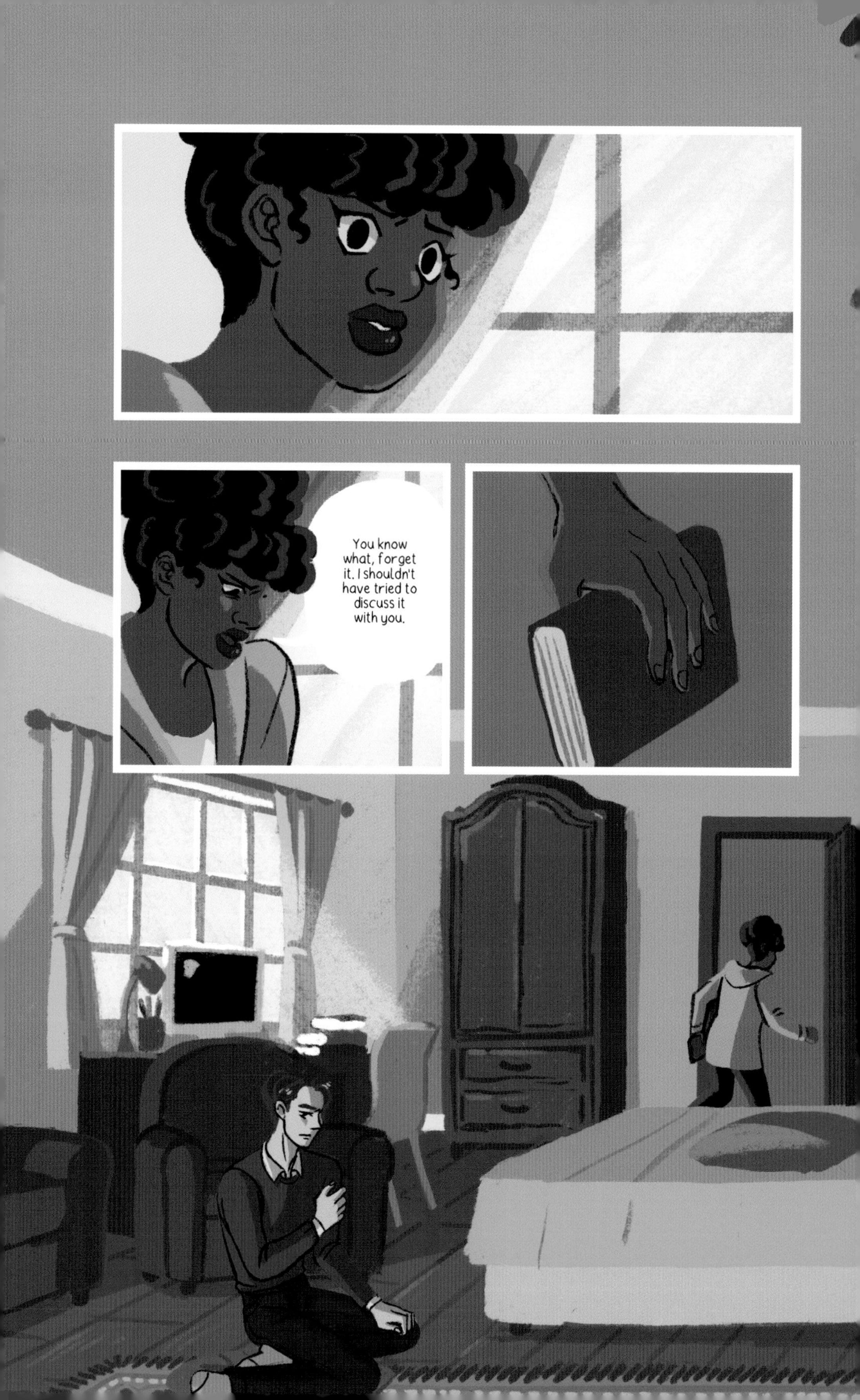
You know what, forget it. I shouldn't have tried to discuss it with you.

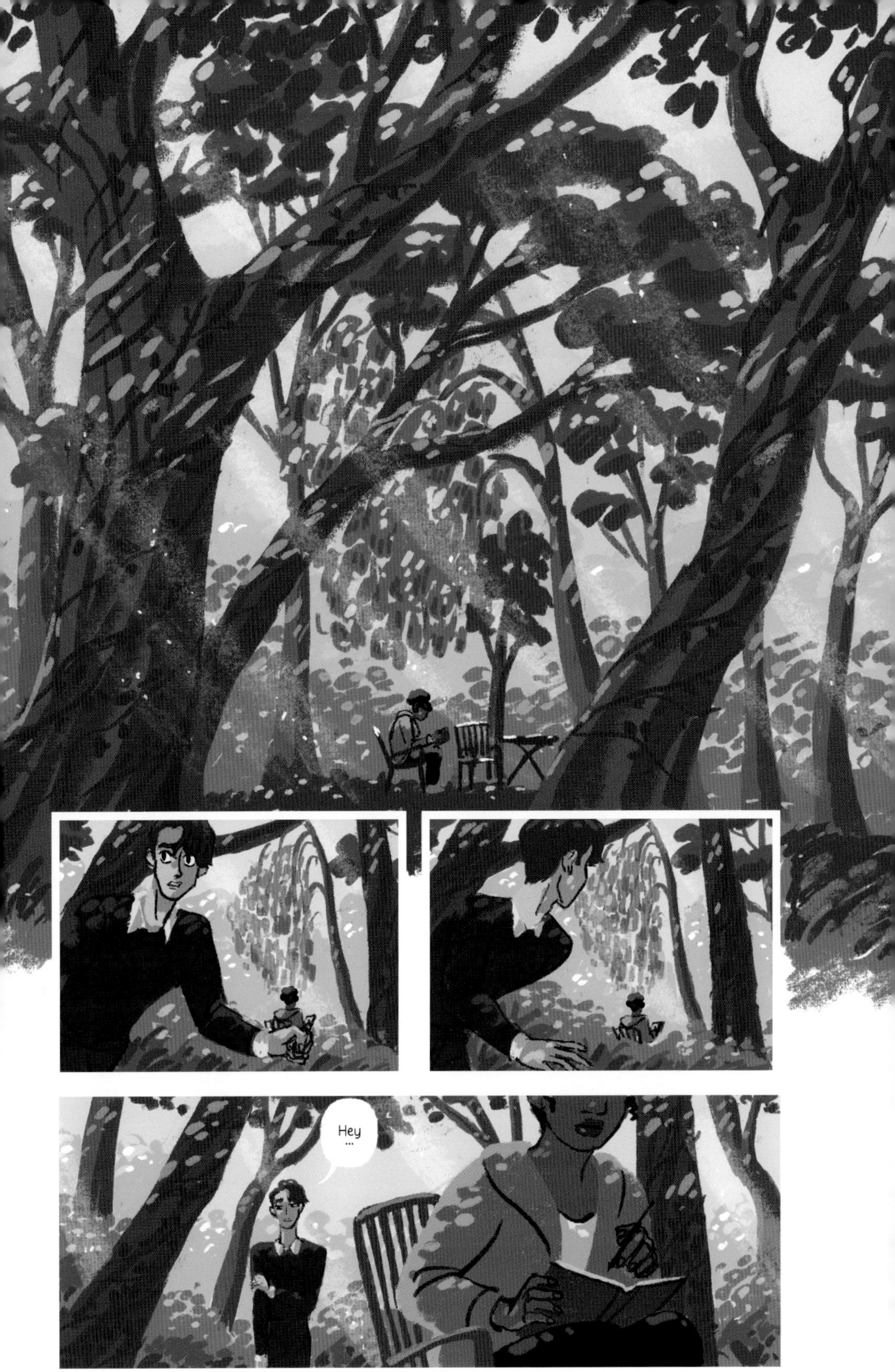
Hey
...

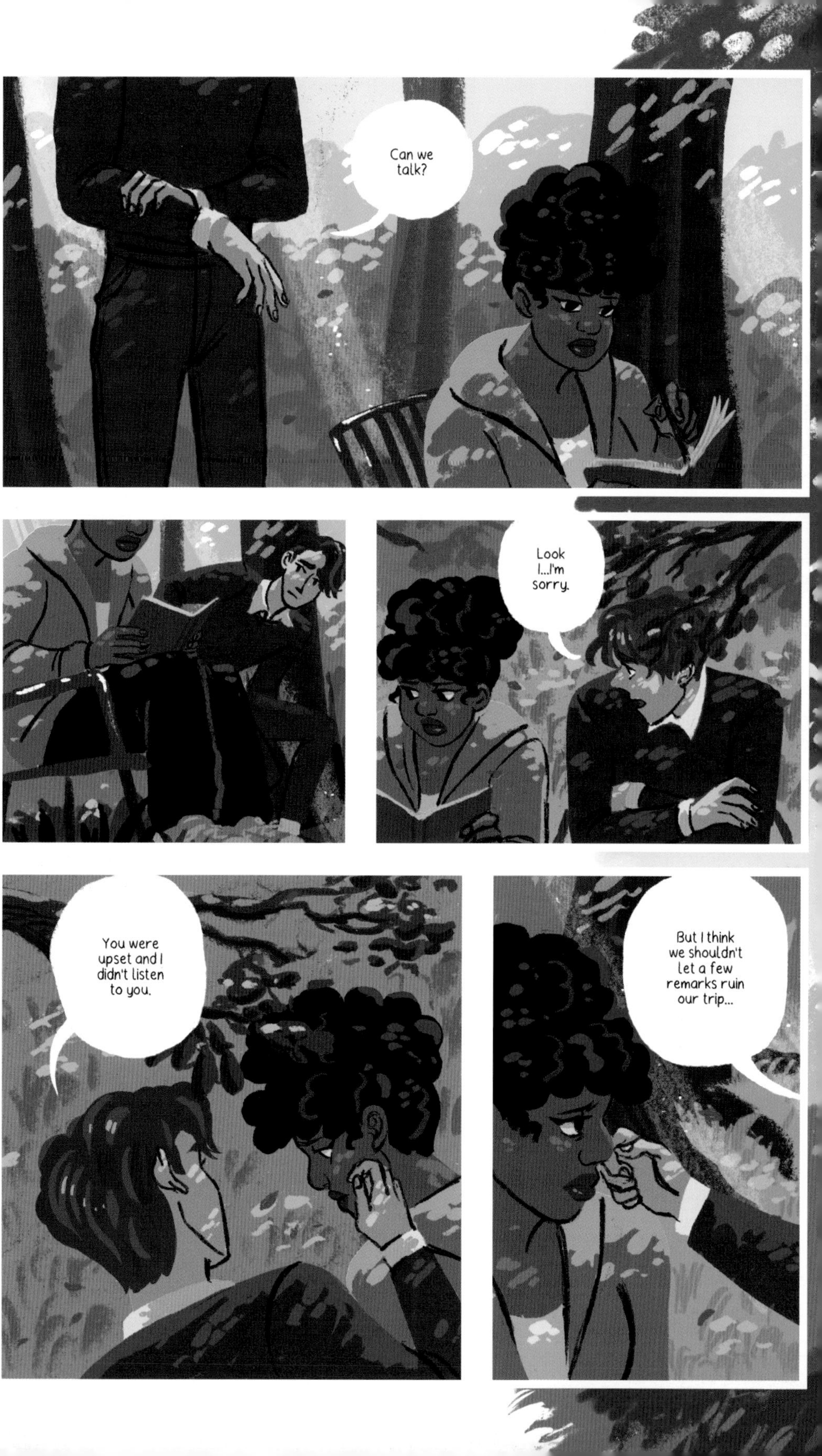
Can we talk?
Look I...I'm sorry.
You were upset and I didn't listen to you.
But I think we shouldn't let a few remarks ruin our trip...

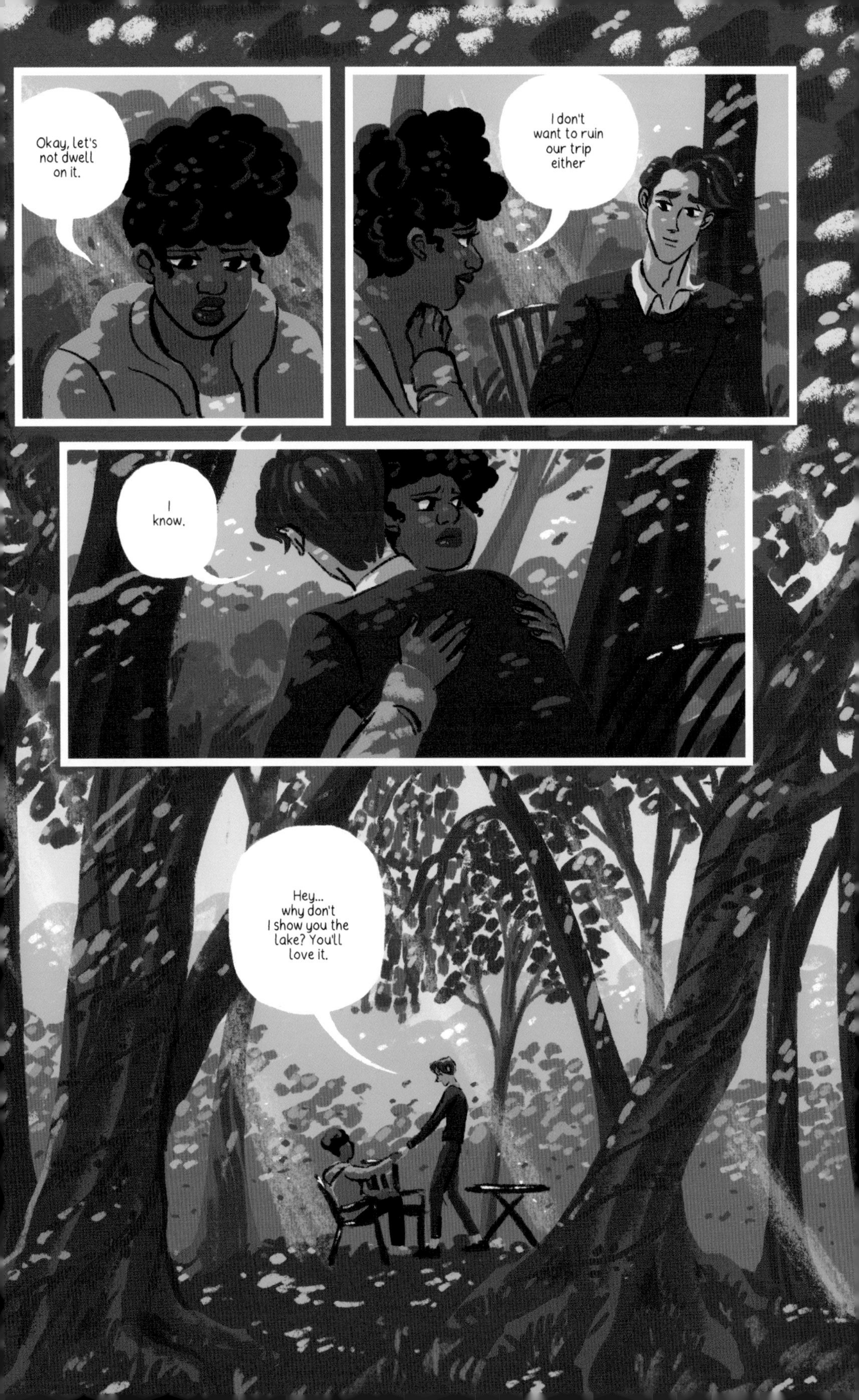
Okay, let's not dwell on it.
I don't want to ruin our trip either
I know.
Hey... why don't I show you the lake? You'll love it.

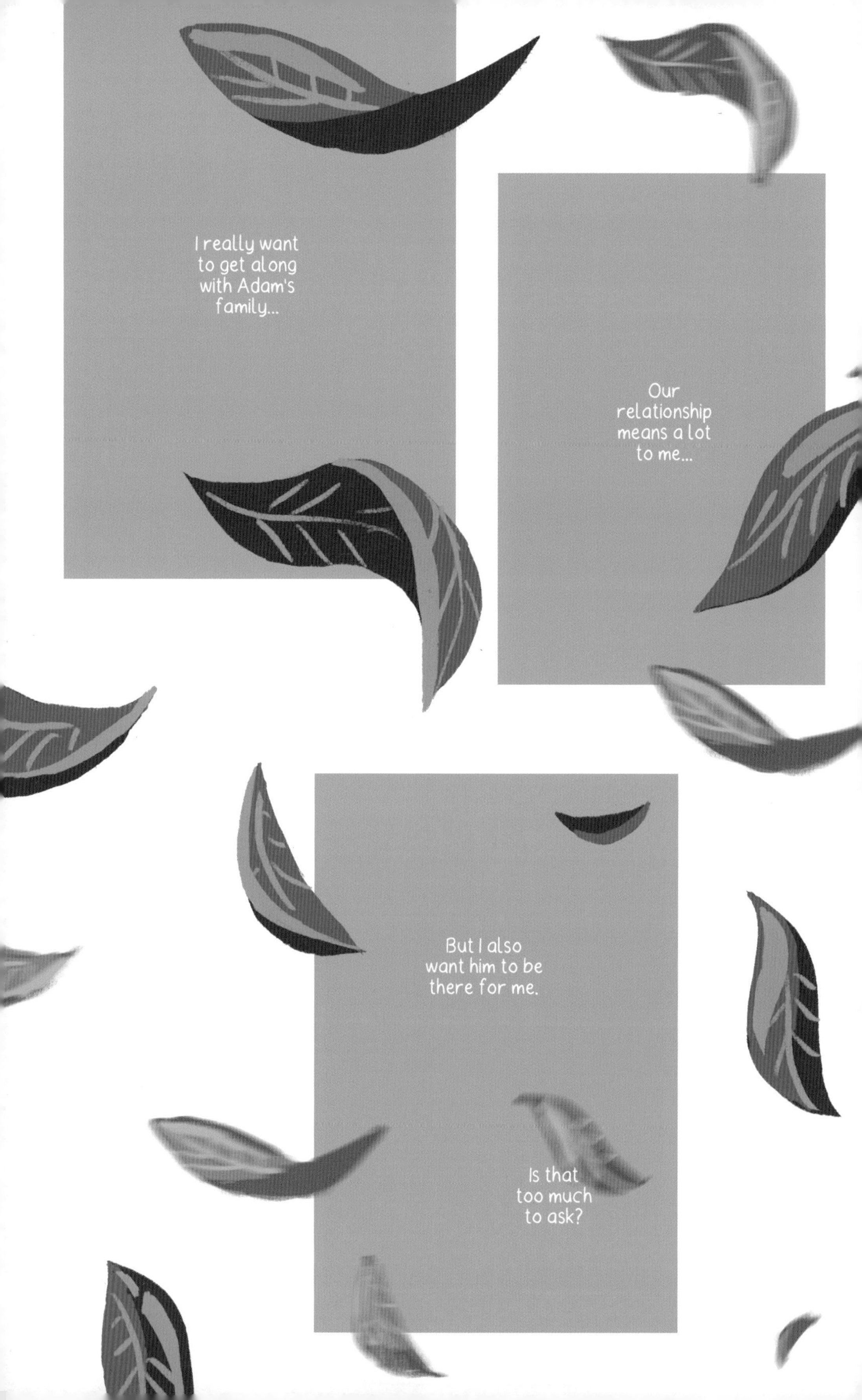
I really want to get along with Adam's family...
Our relationship means a lot to me...
But I also want him to be there for me.
Is that too much to ask?

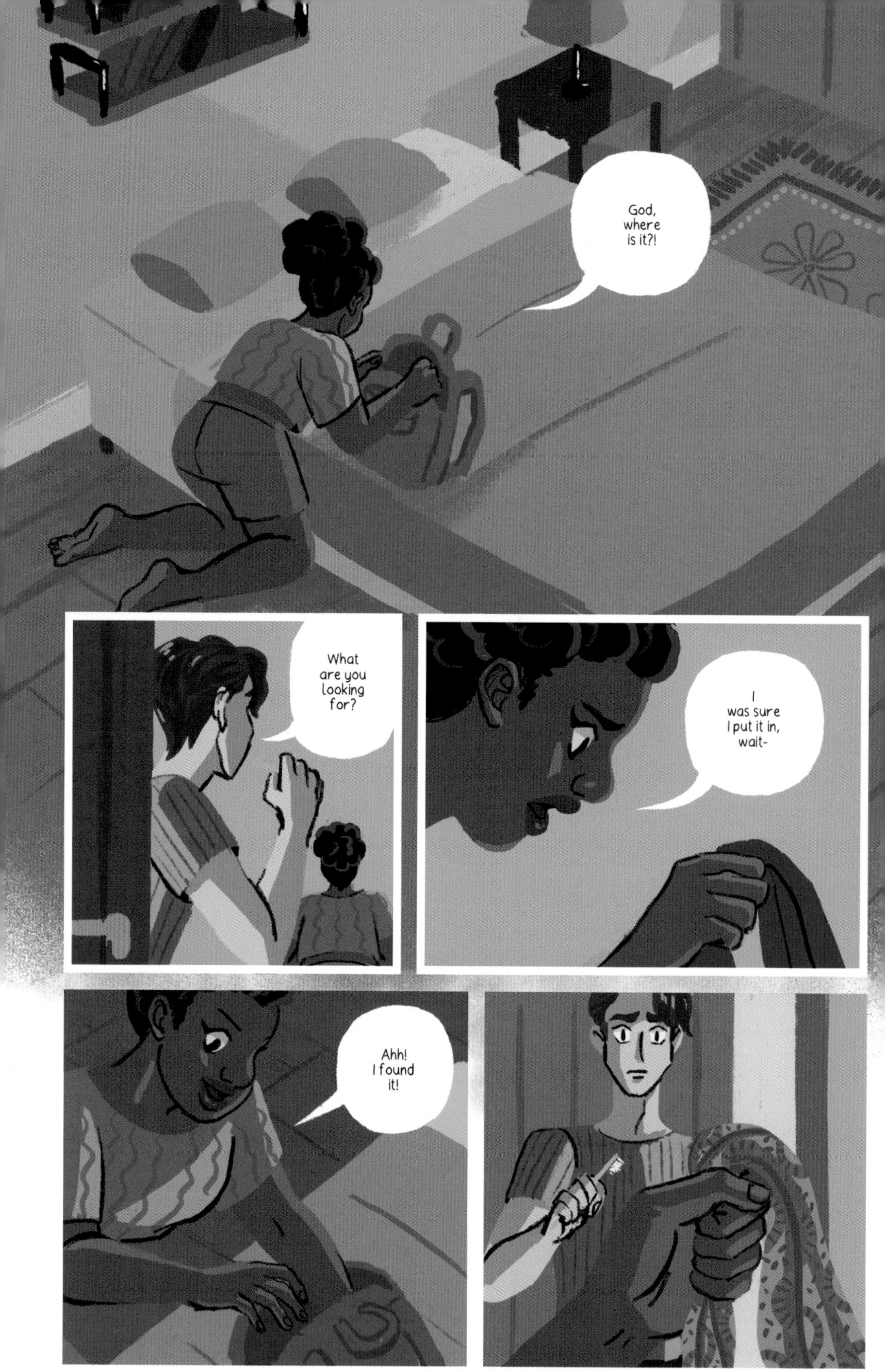
God, where is it?!
What are you looking for?
I was sure I put it in, wait-
Ahh! I found it!

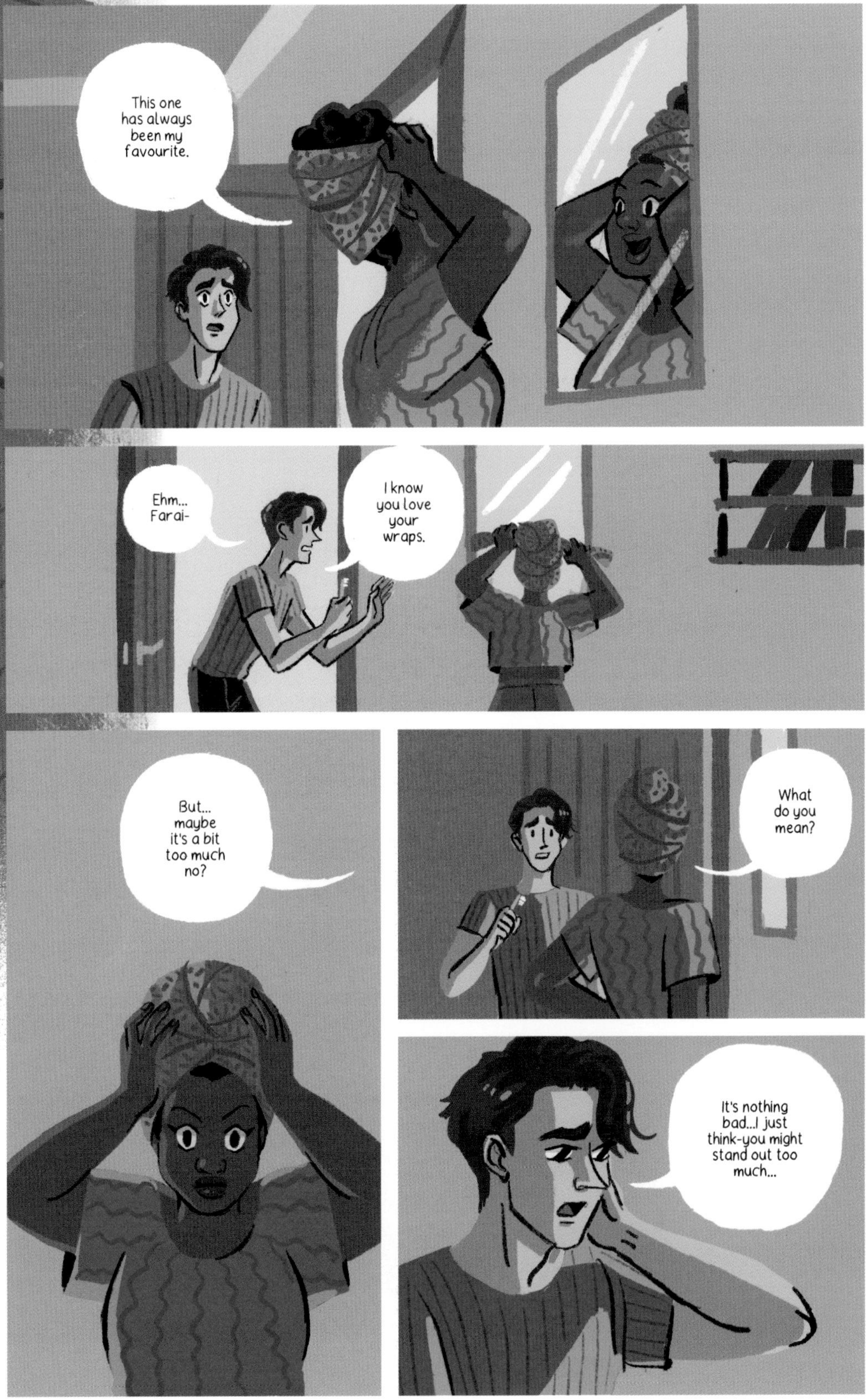
This one has always been my favourite.
Ehm... Farai-
I know you love your wraps.
But... maybe it's a bit too much no?
What do you mean?
It's nothing bad...I just think-you might stand out too much...

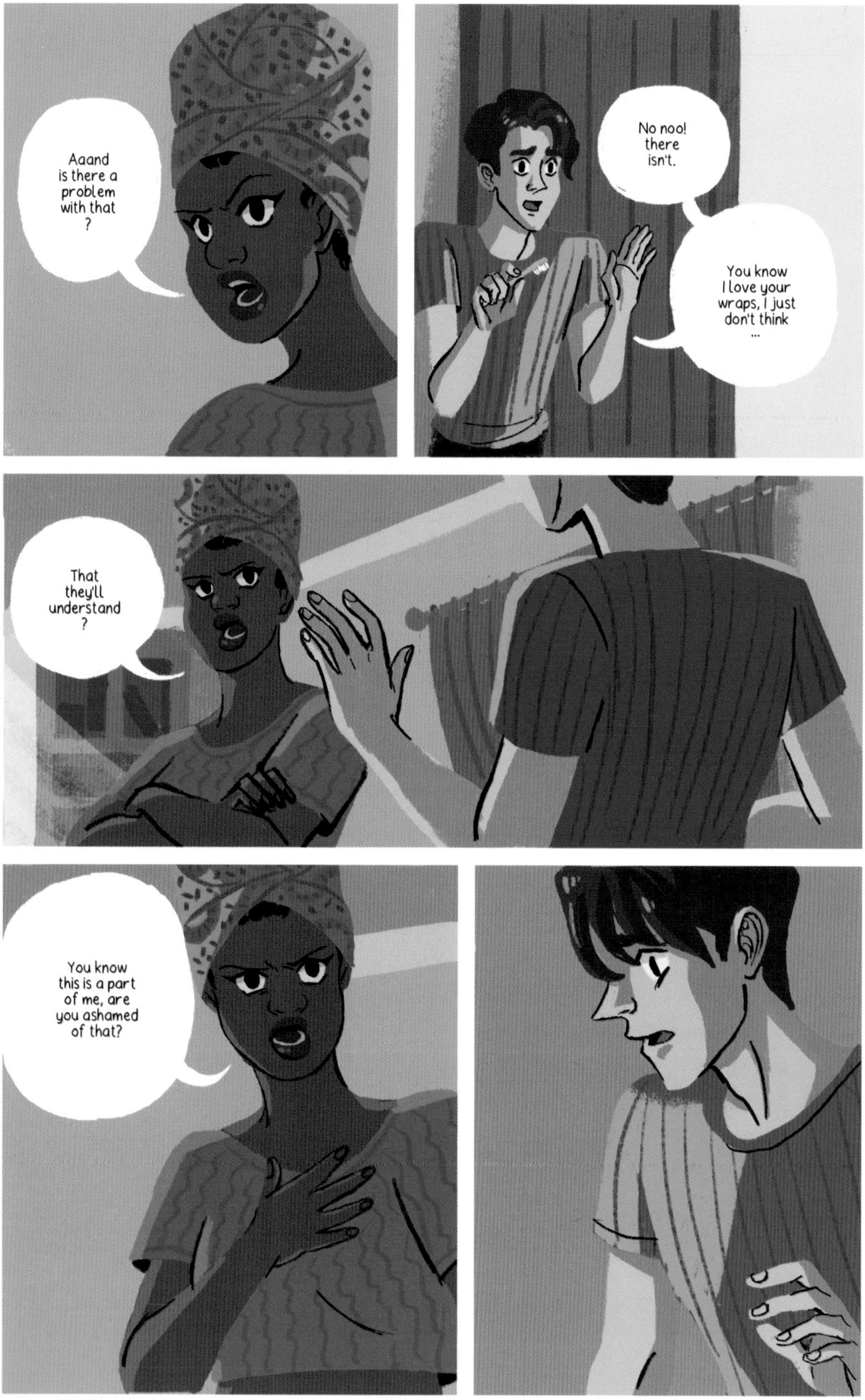
Aaand is there a problem with that ?
No noo! there isn't.
You know I love your wraps, I just don't think ...
That they'll understand ?
You know this is a part of me, are you ashamed of that?

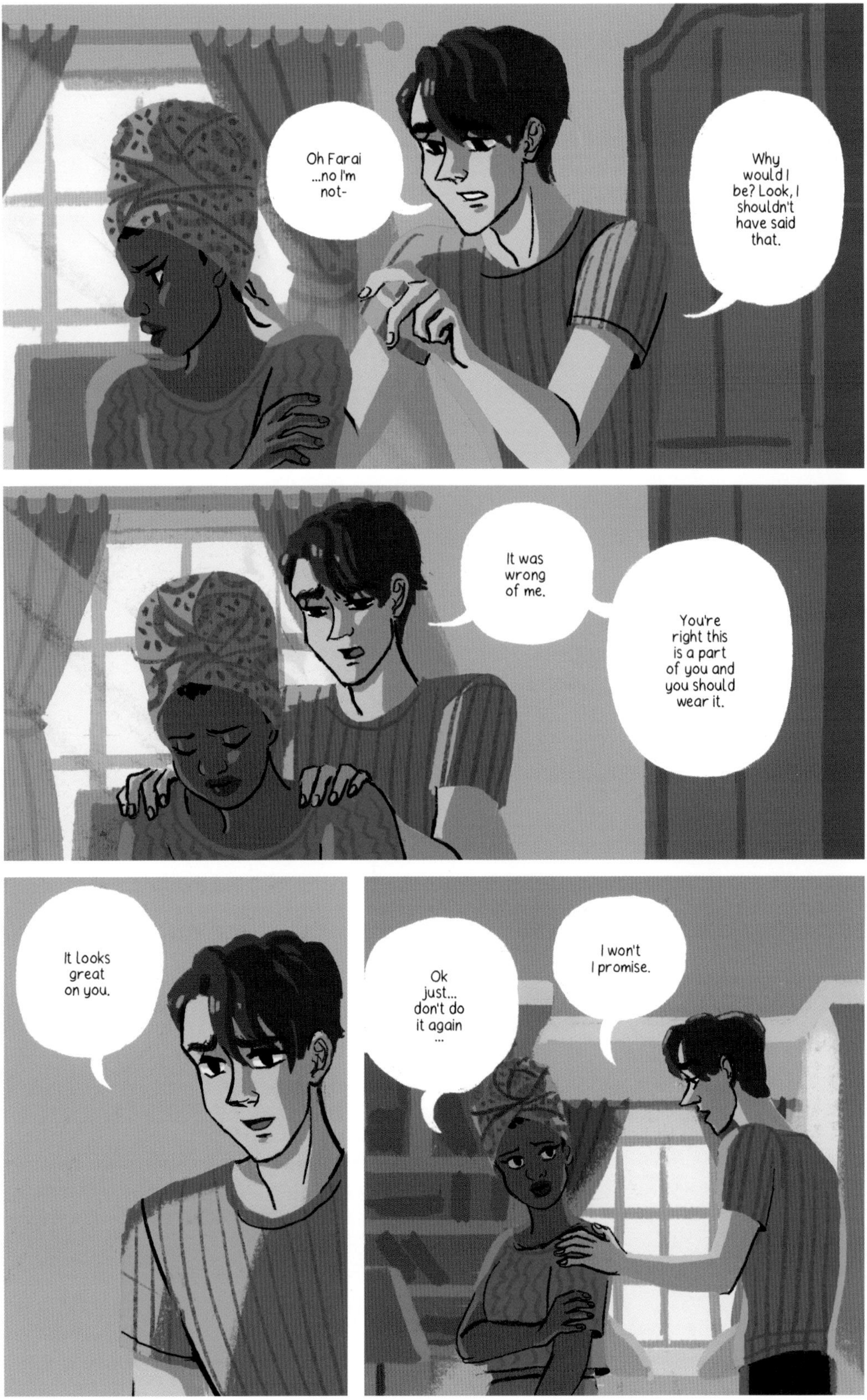

Oh Farai ...no I'm not-
Why would I be? Look, I shouldn't have said that.
It was wrong of me.
You're right this is a part of you and you should wear it.
It looks great on you.
Ok just... don't do it again ...
I won't I promise.

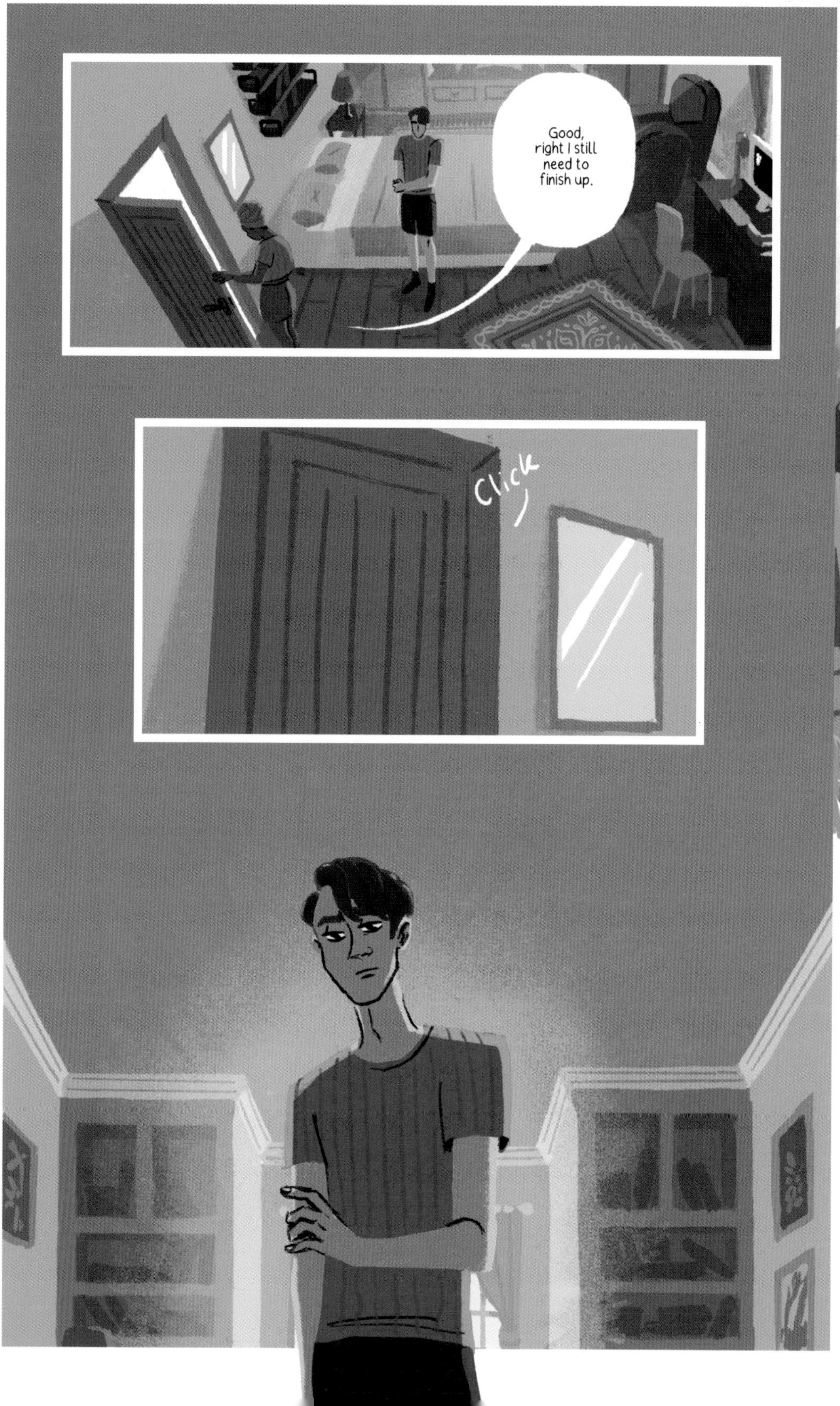
Good, right I still need to finish up.
Click

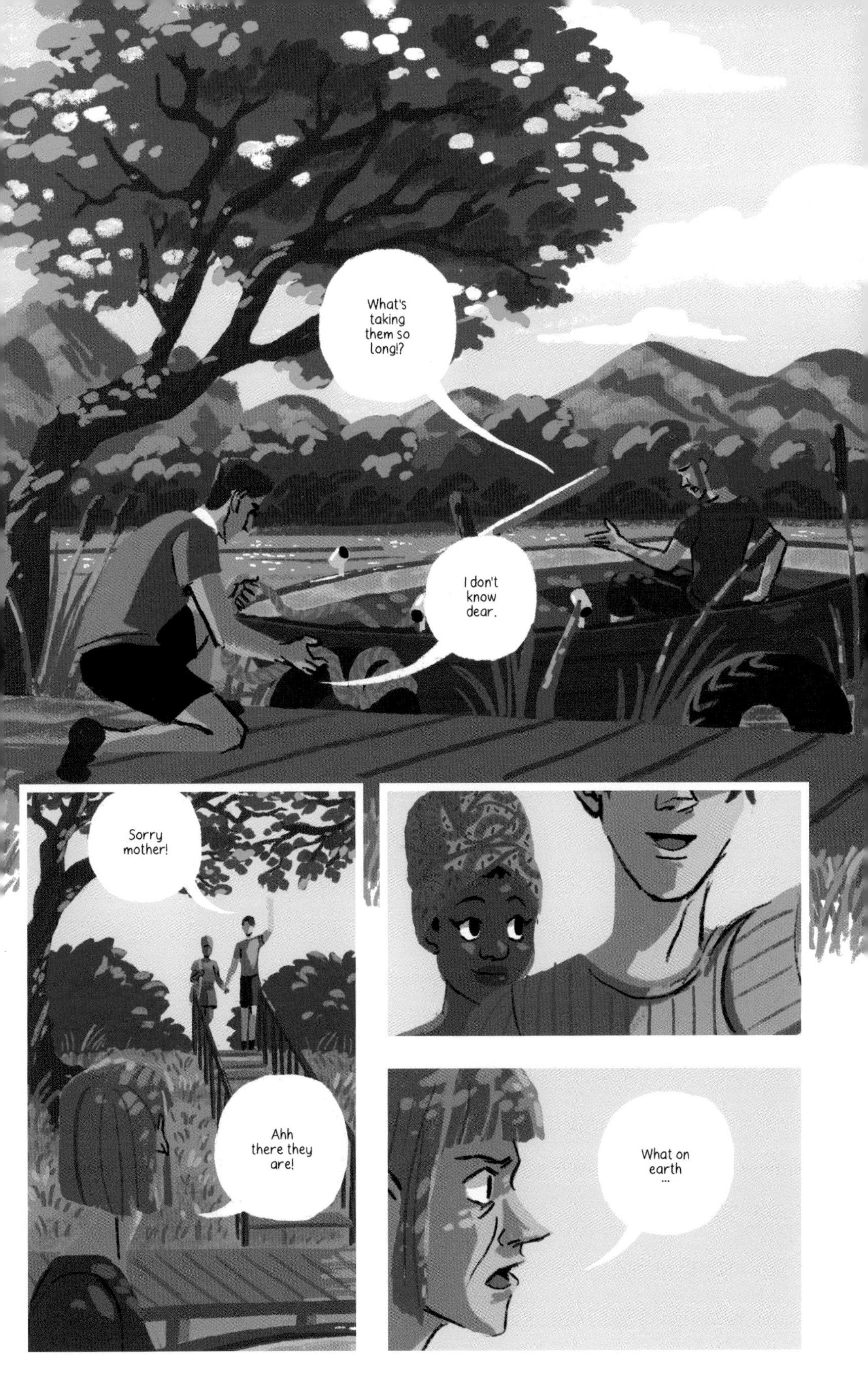
What's taking them so long!?
I don't know dear.
Sorry mother!
Ahh there they are!
What on earth ...

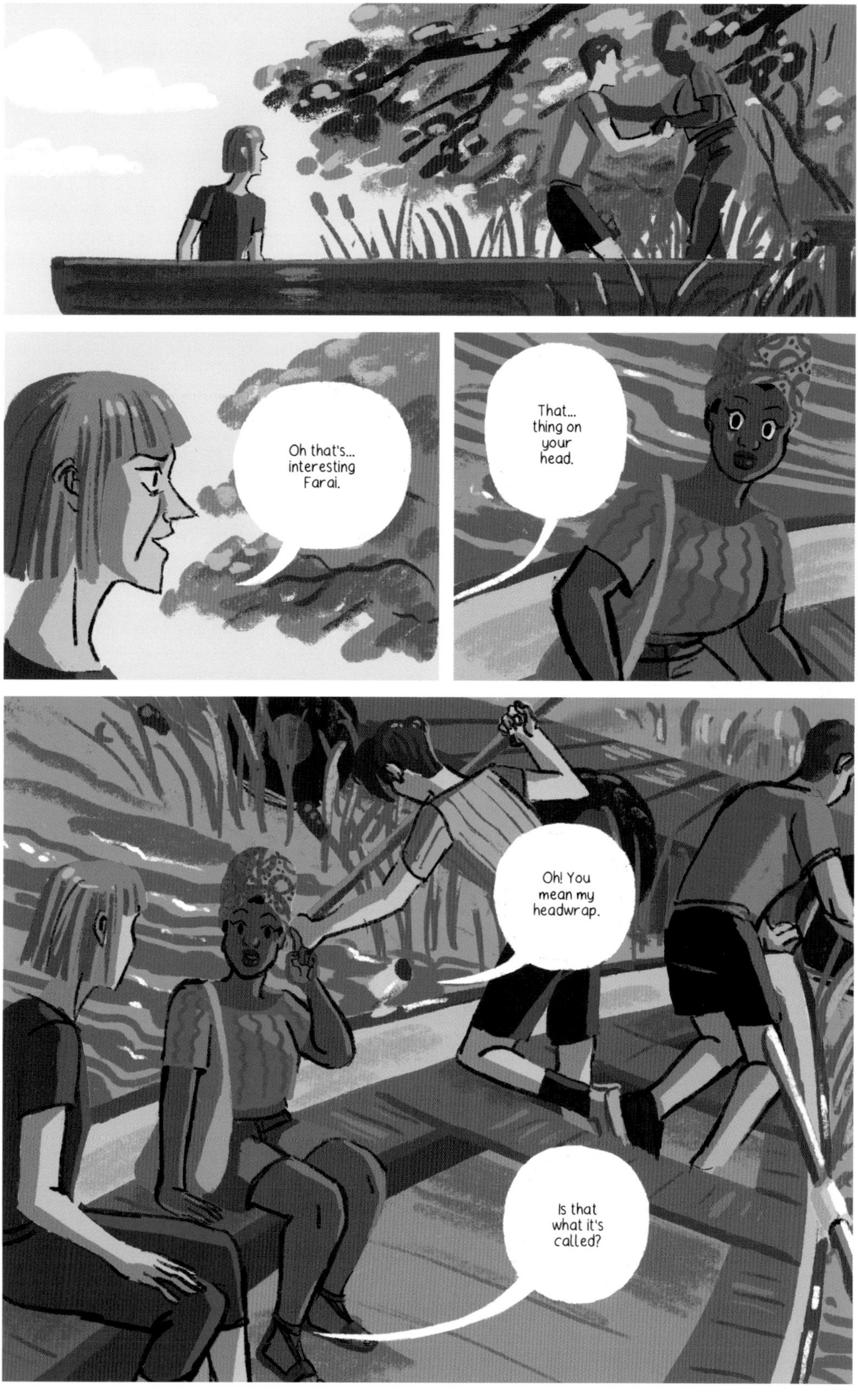
Oh that's... interesting Farai.
That... thing on your head.
Oh! You mean my headwrap.
Is that what it's called?

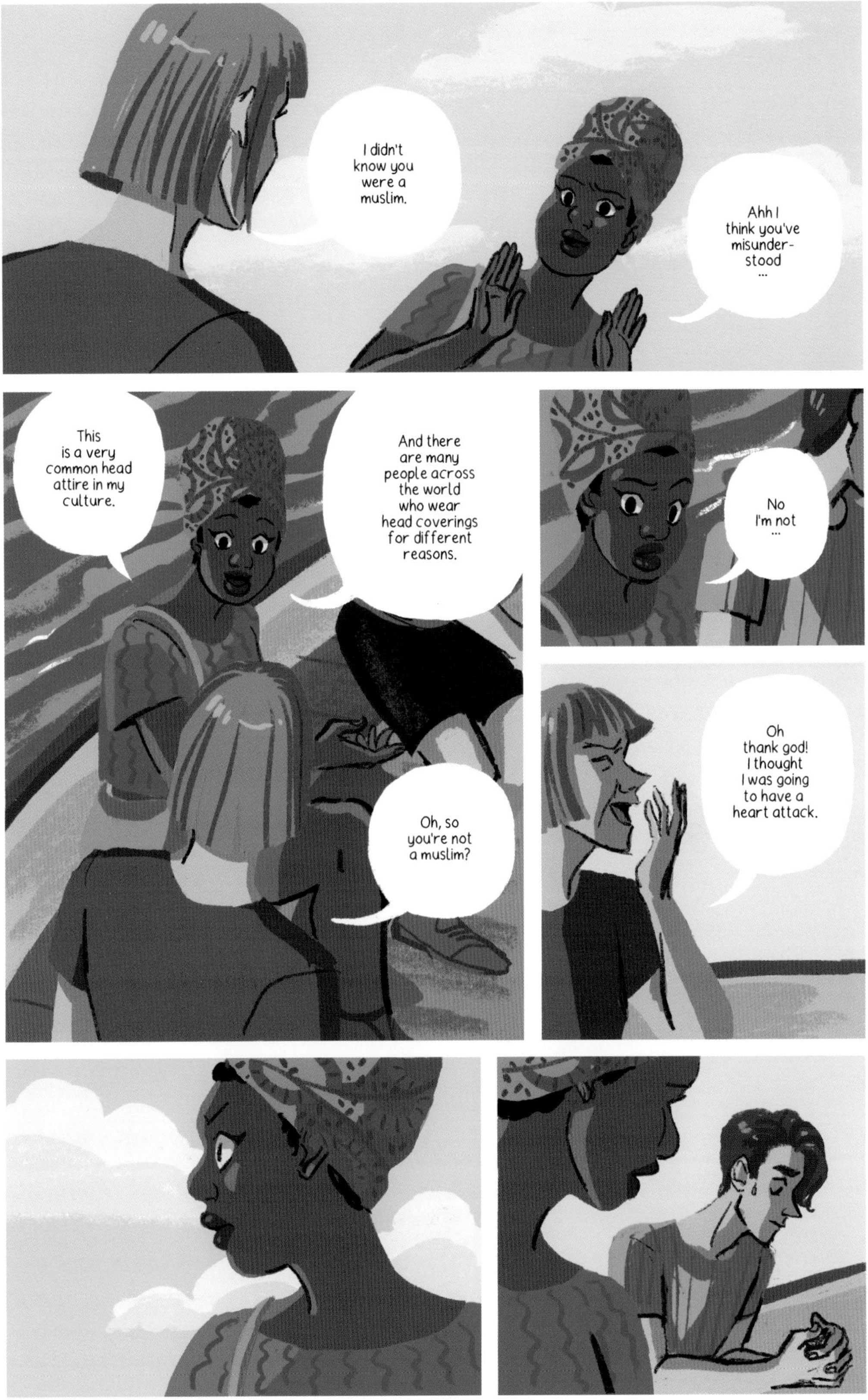
I didn't know you were a muslim.
Ahh I think you've misunder-stood ...
This is a very common head attire in my culture.
And there are many people across the world who wear head coverings for different reasons.
Oh, so you're not a muslim?
No I'm not ...
Oh thank god! I thought I was going to have a heart attack.

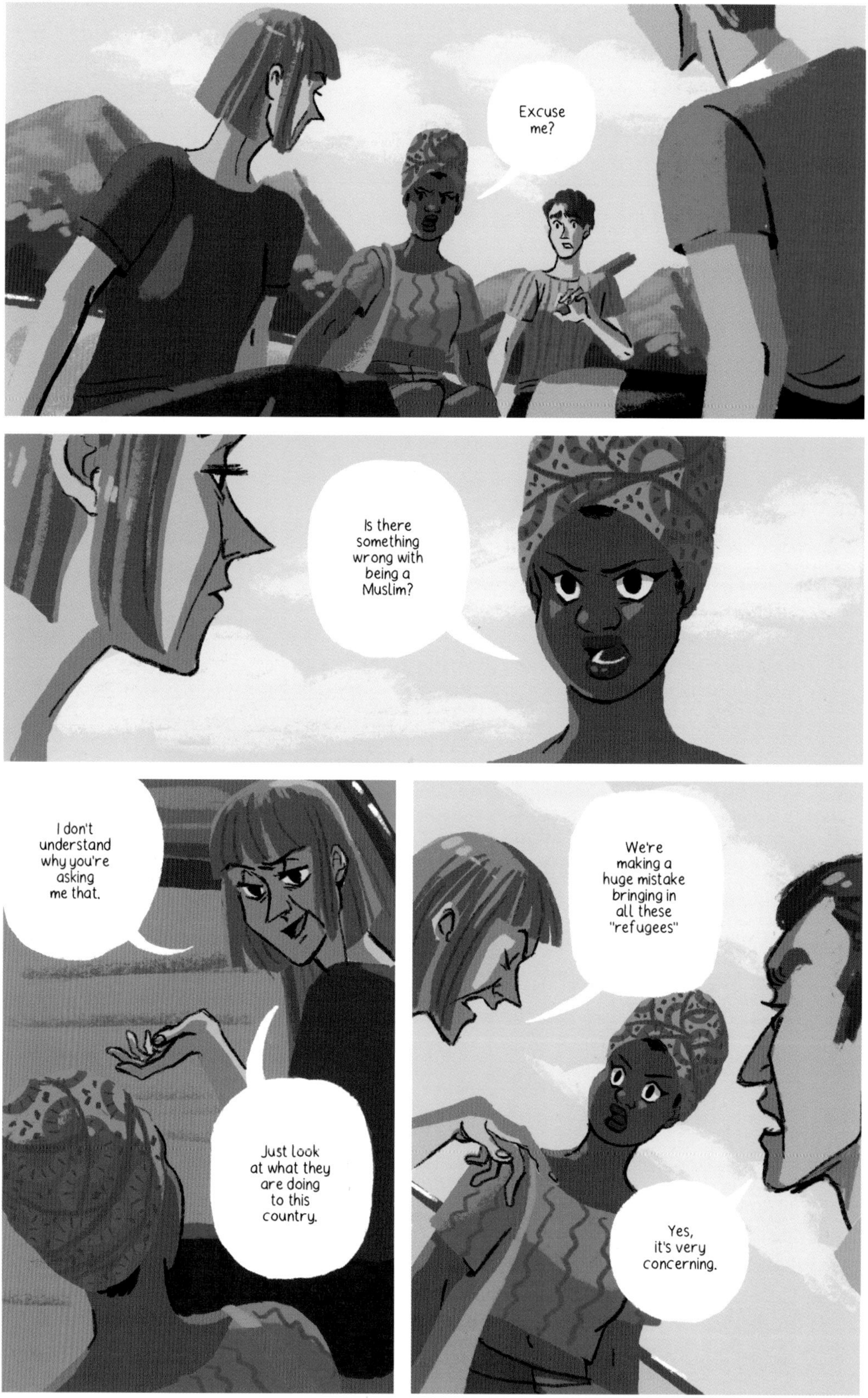
Excuse me?
Is there something wrong with being a Muslim?
I don't understand why you're asking me that.
Just look at what they are doing to this country.
We're making a huge mistake bringing in all these "refugees"
Yes, it's very concerning.

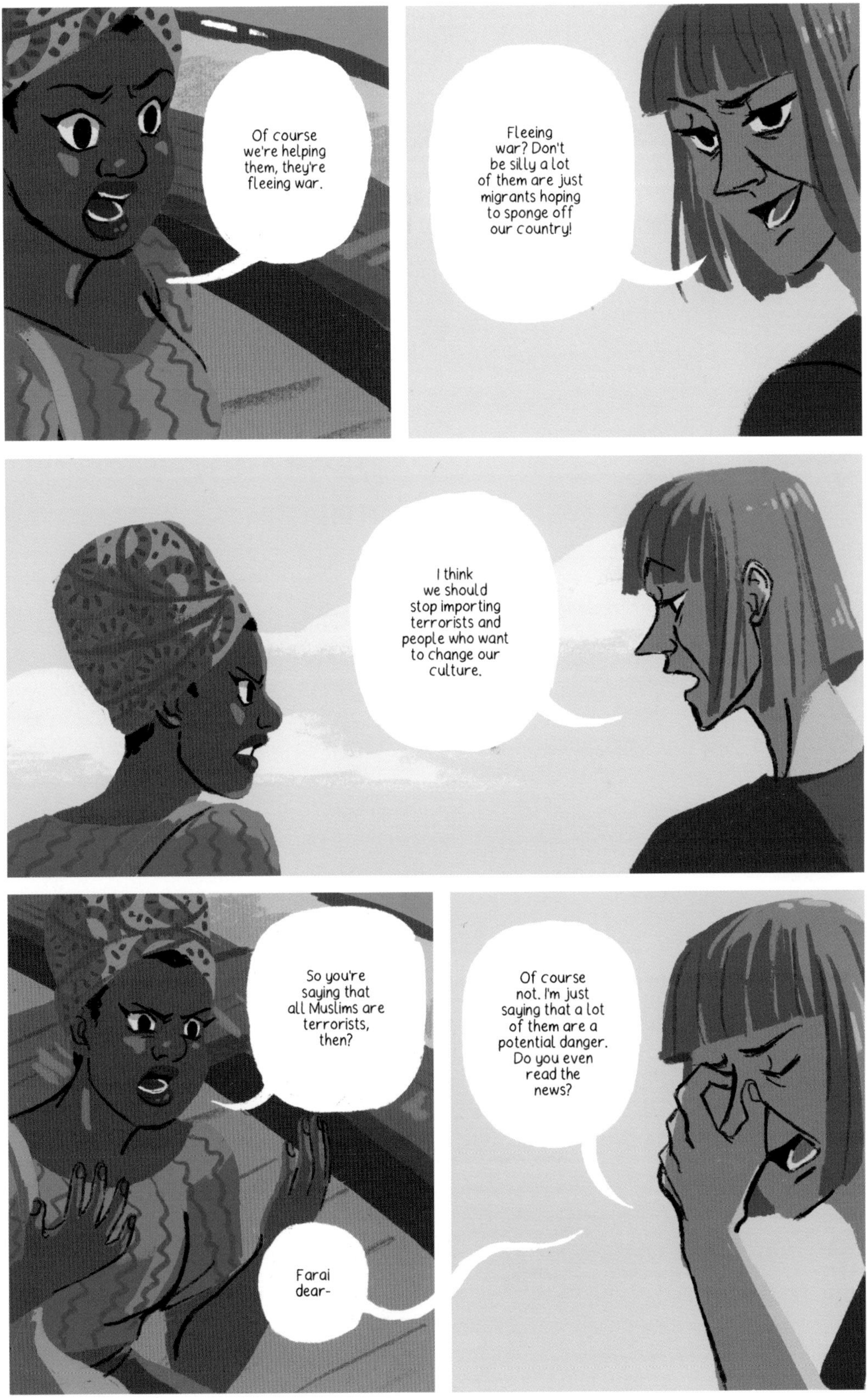
Of course we're helping them, they're fleeing war.
Fleeing war? Don't be silly a lot of them are just migrants hoping to sponge off our country!
I think we should stop importing terrorists and people who want to change our culture.
So you're saying that all Muslims are terrorists, then?
Of course not. I'm just saying that a lot of them are a potential danger. Do you even read the news?
Farai dear-

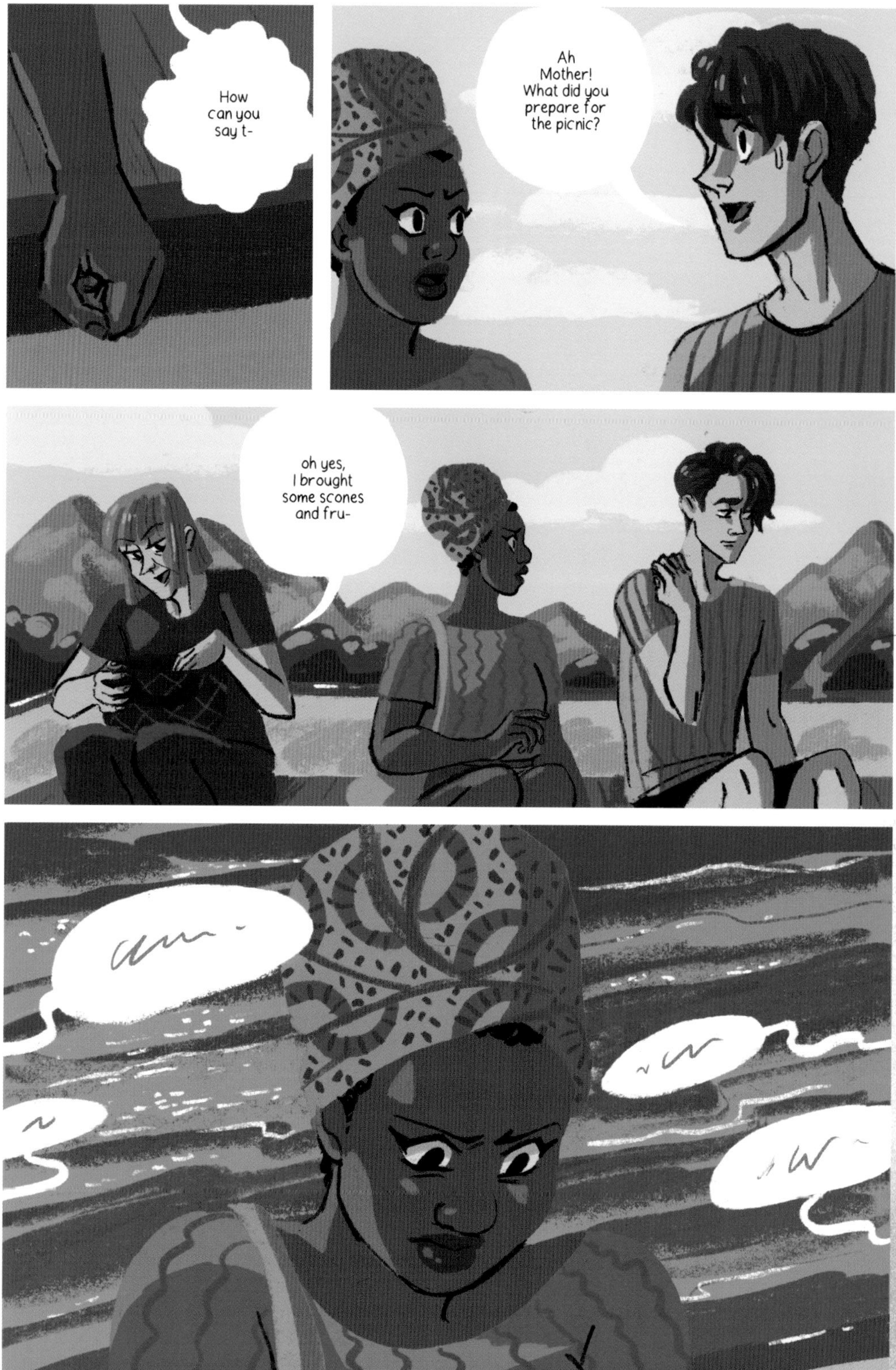
How can you say t-
Ah Mother! What did you prepare for the picnic?
oh yes, I brought some scones and fru-

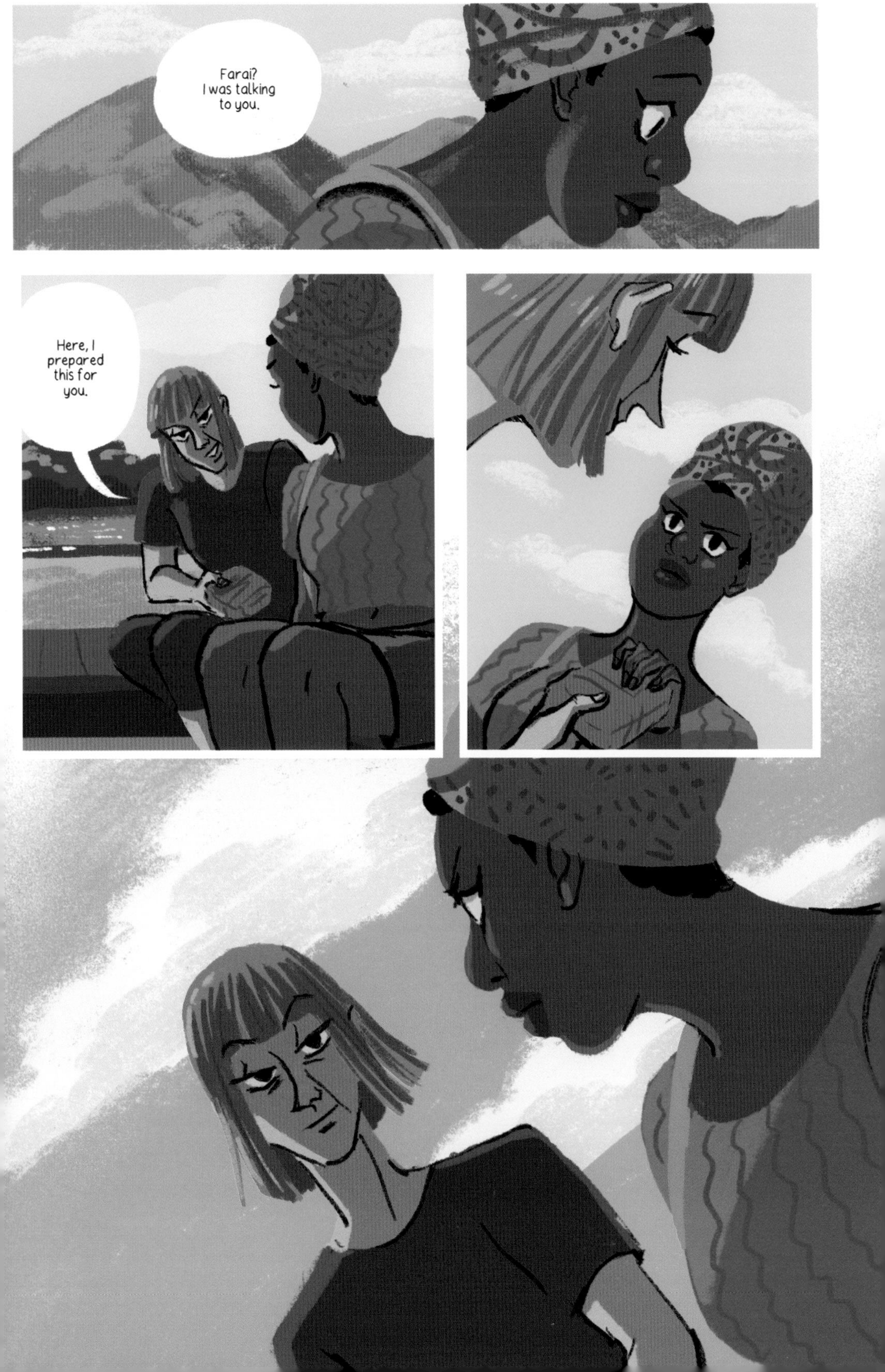
Farai? I was talking to you.
Here, I prepared this for you.

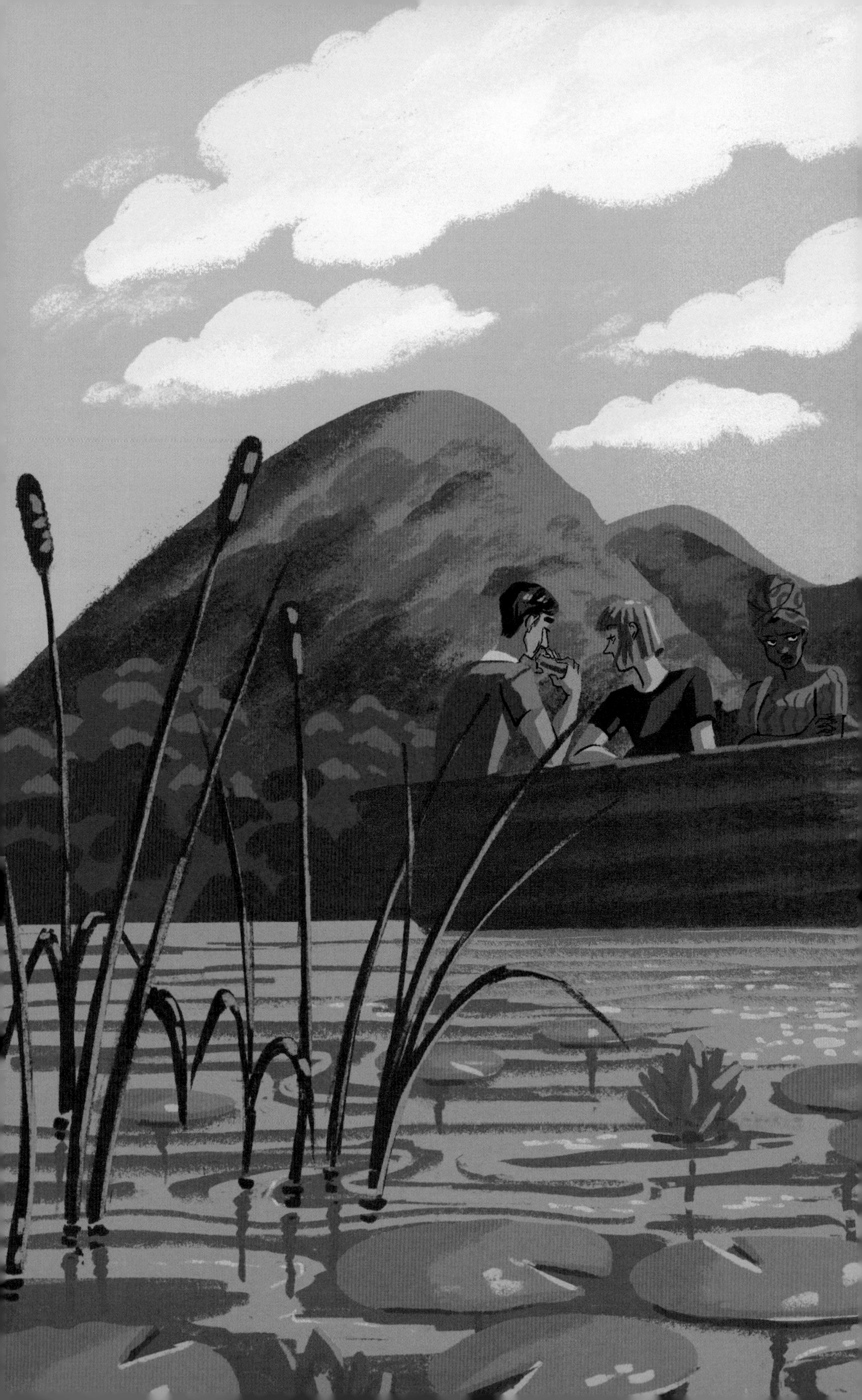

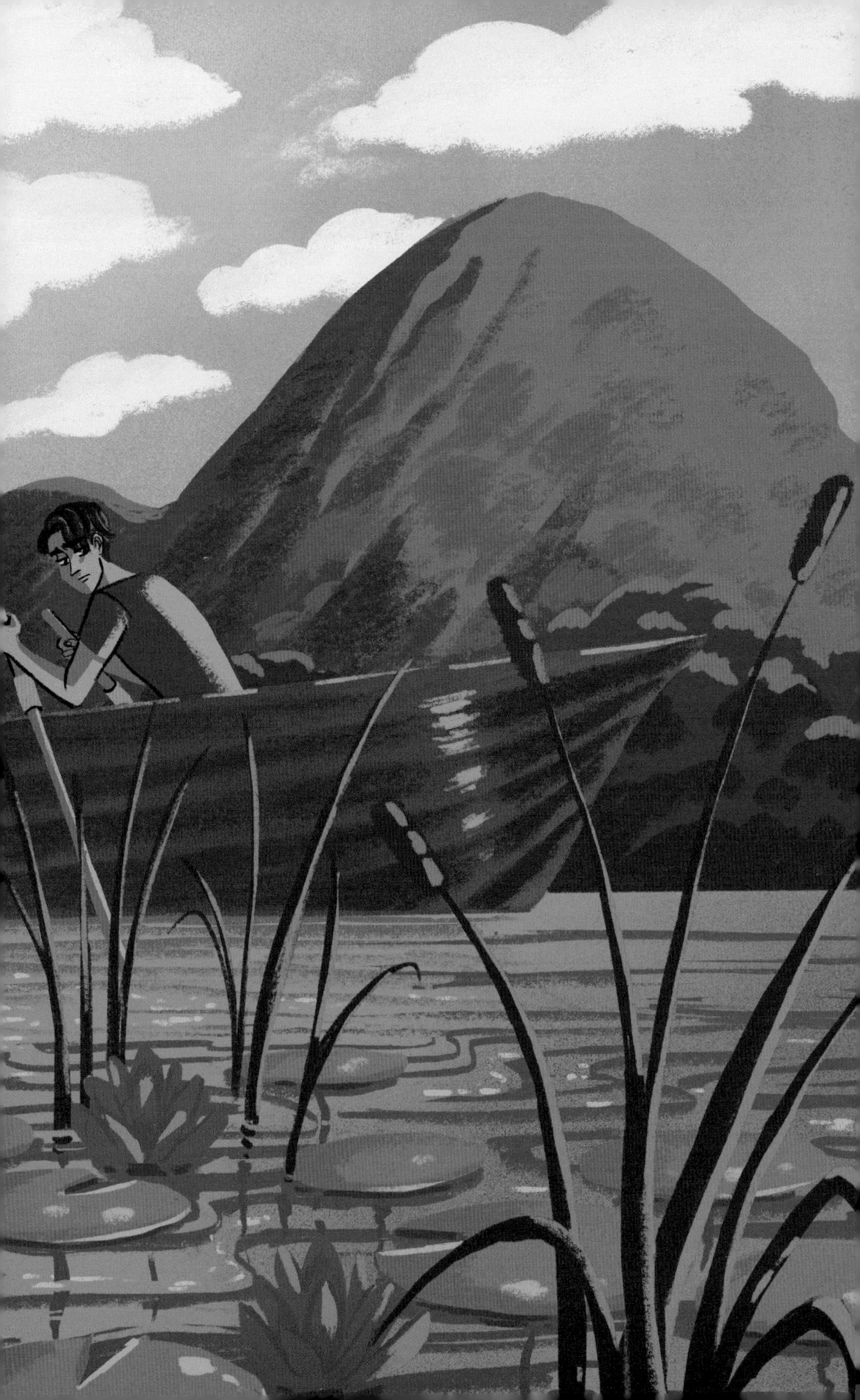

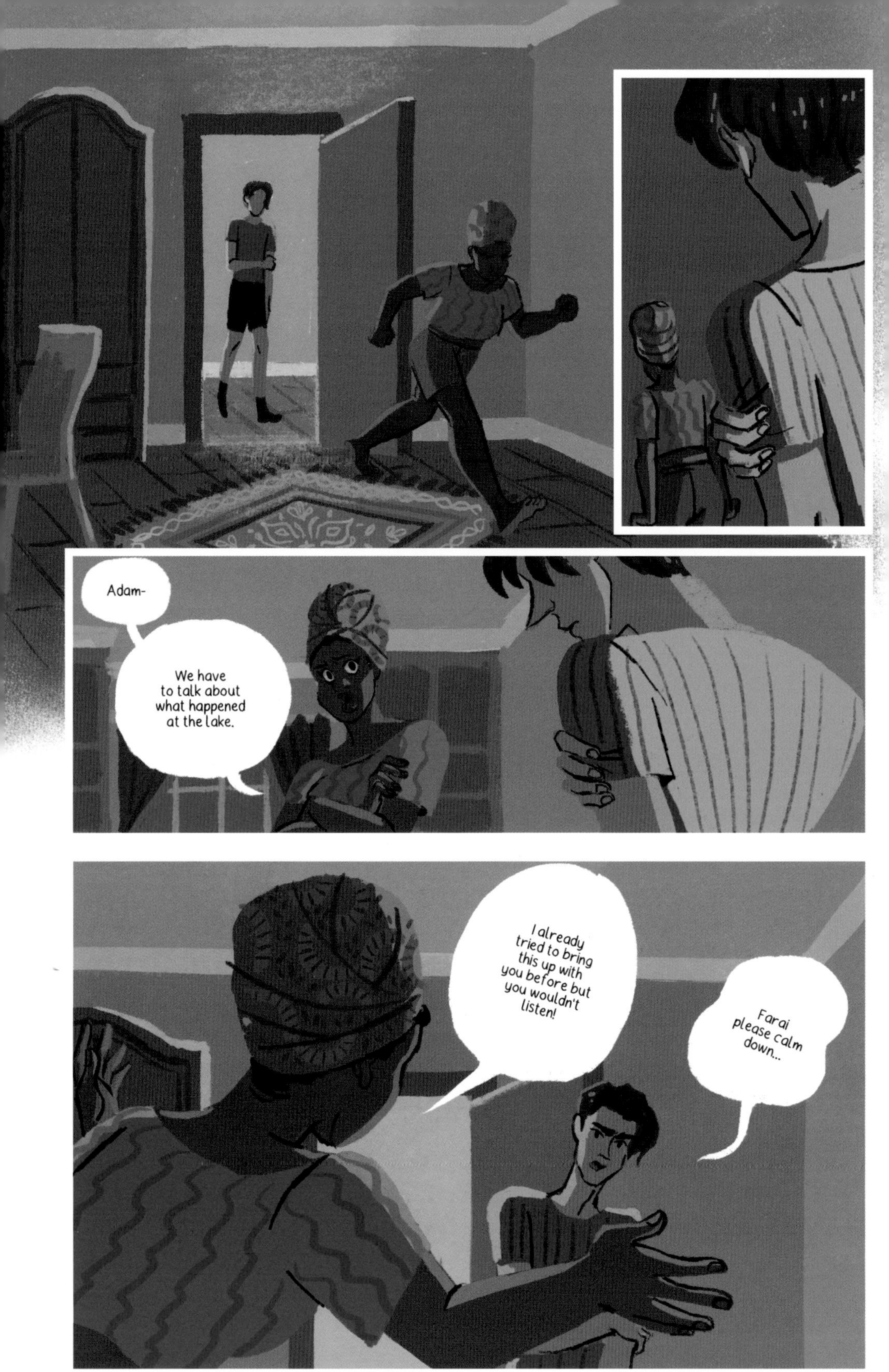
Adam-
We have to talk about what happened at the lake.
I already tried to bring this up with you before but you wouldn't listen!
Farai please calm down...

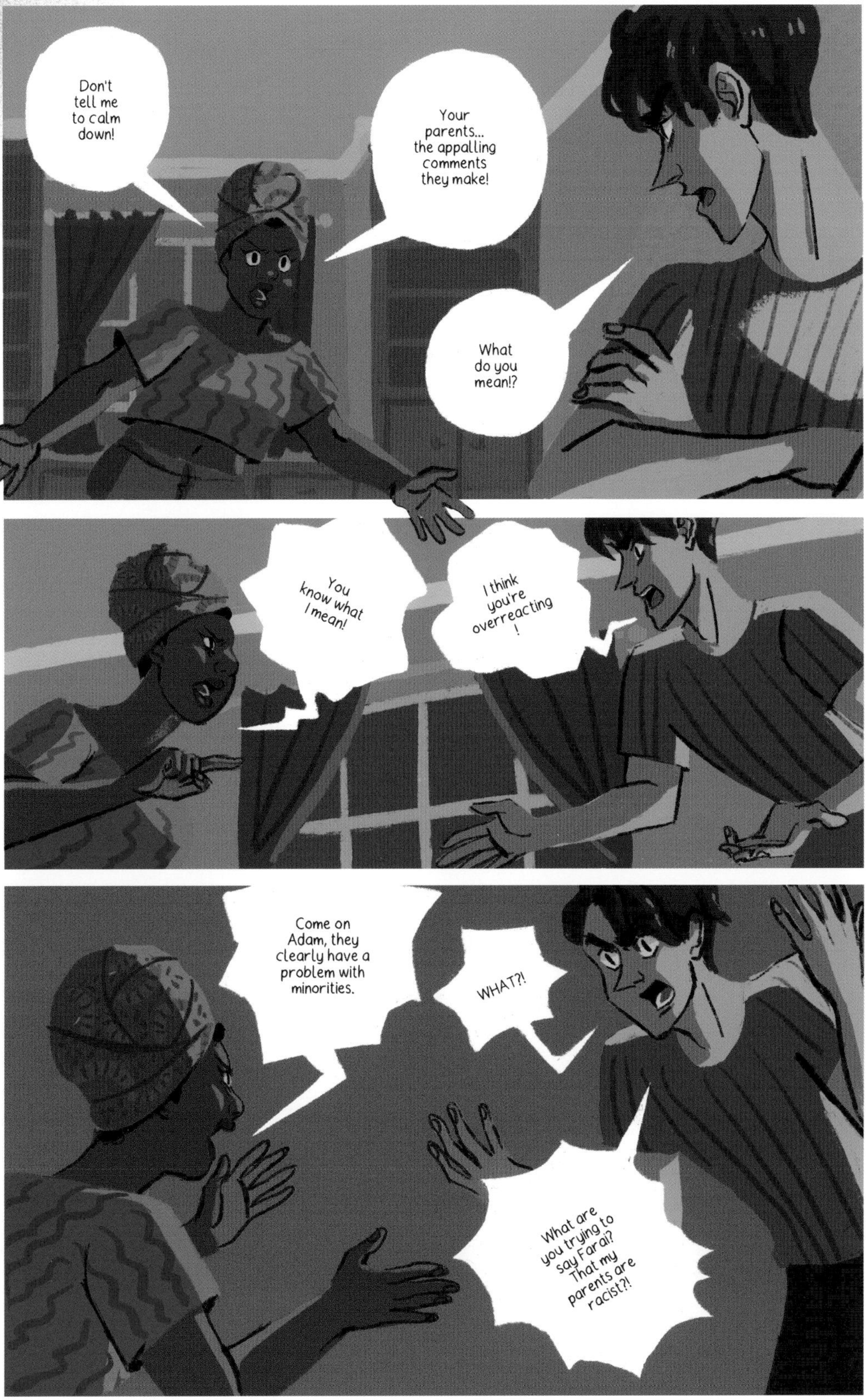
Don't tell me to calm down!
Your parents... the appalling comments they make!
What do you mean!?
You know what I mean!
I think you're overreacting!
Come on Adam, they clearly have a problem with minorities.
WHAT?!
What are you trying to say Farai? That my parents are racist?!

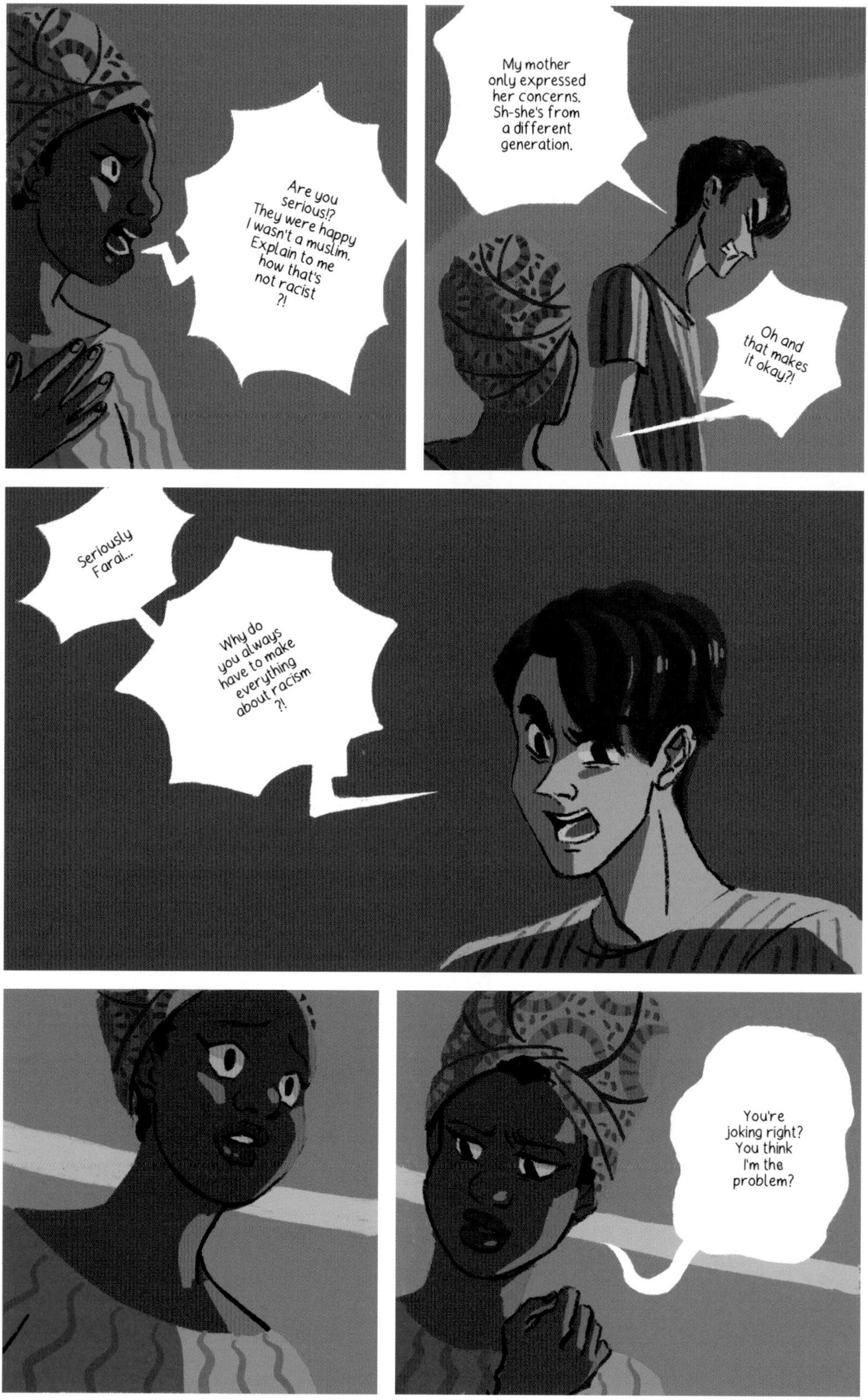
Are you serious!? They were happy I wasn't a muslim. Explain to me how that's not racist ?!
My mother only expressed her concerns. Sh-she's from a different generation.
Oh and that makes it okay?!
Seriously Farai...
Why do you always have to make everything about racism ?!
You're joking right? You think I'm the problem?

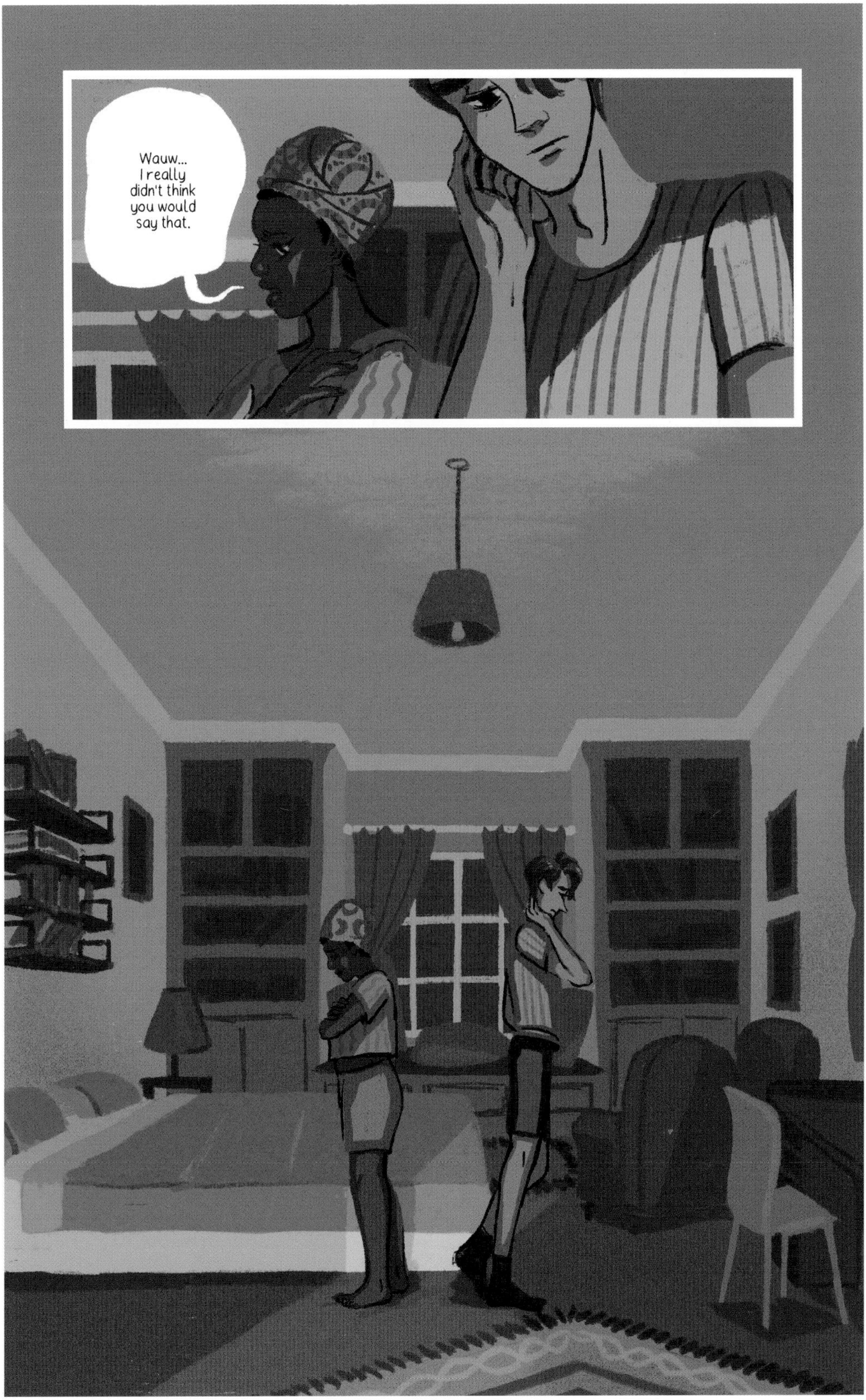
Wauw... I really didn't think you would say that.

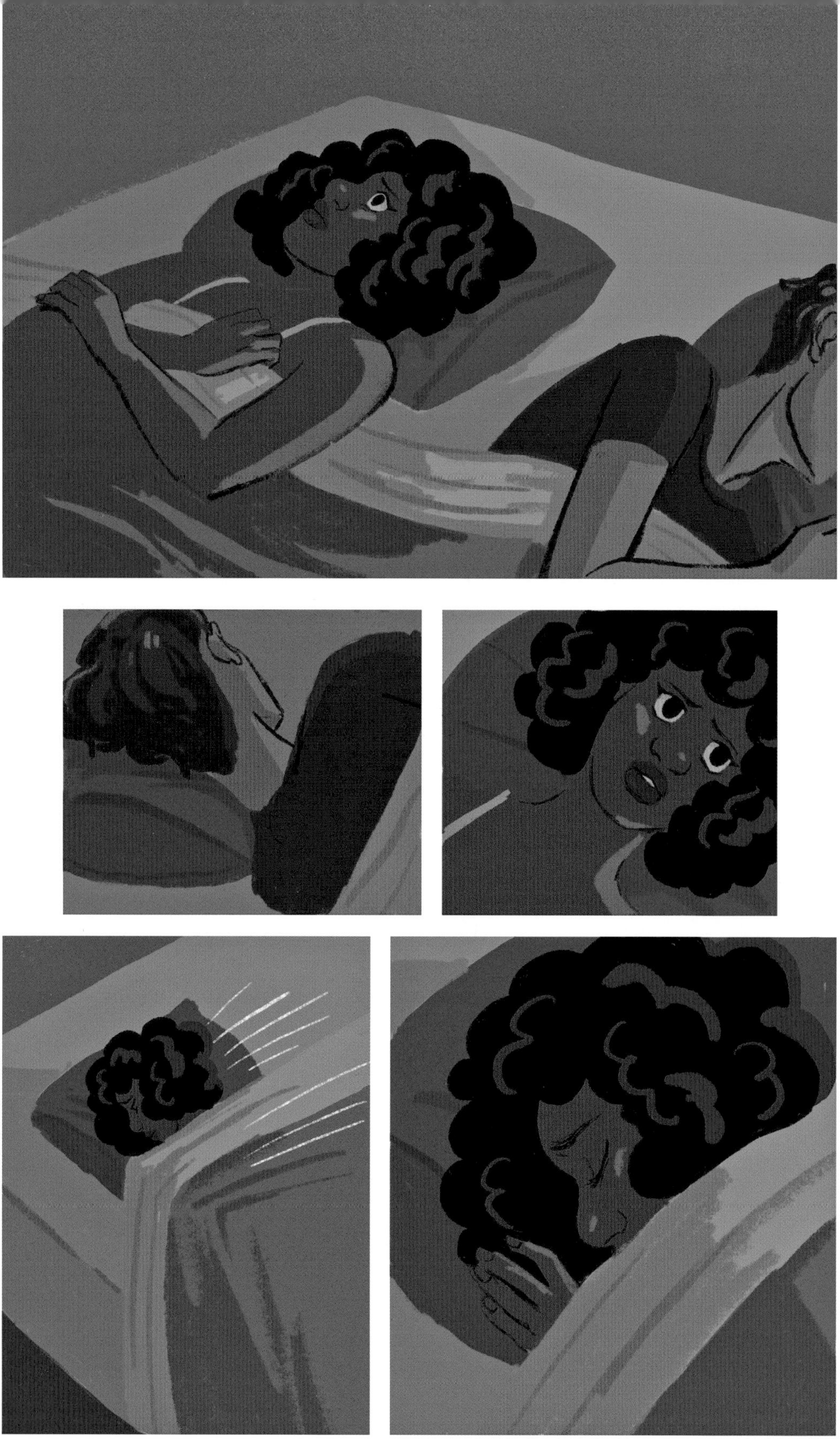

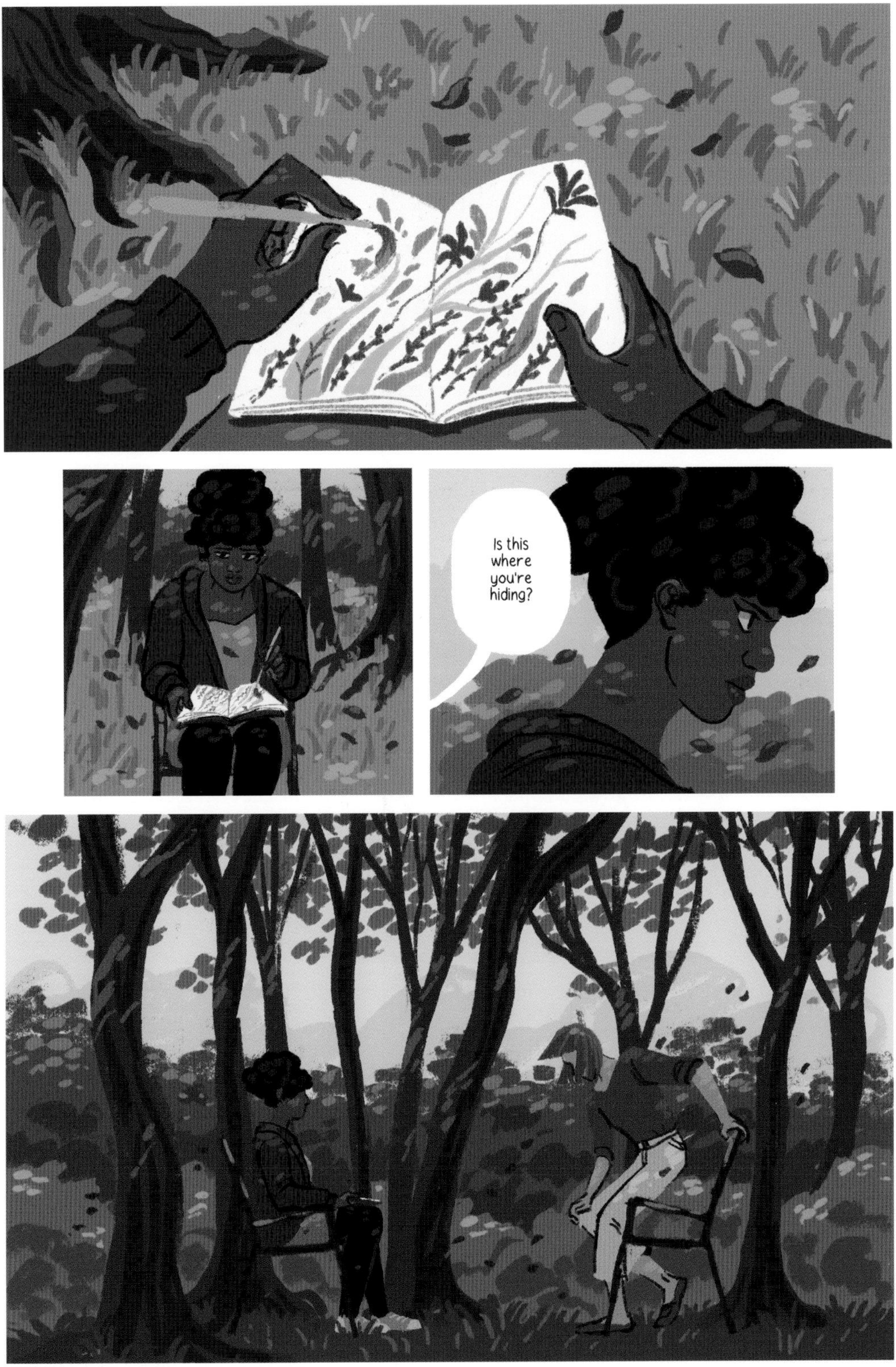
Is this where you're hiding?

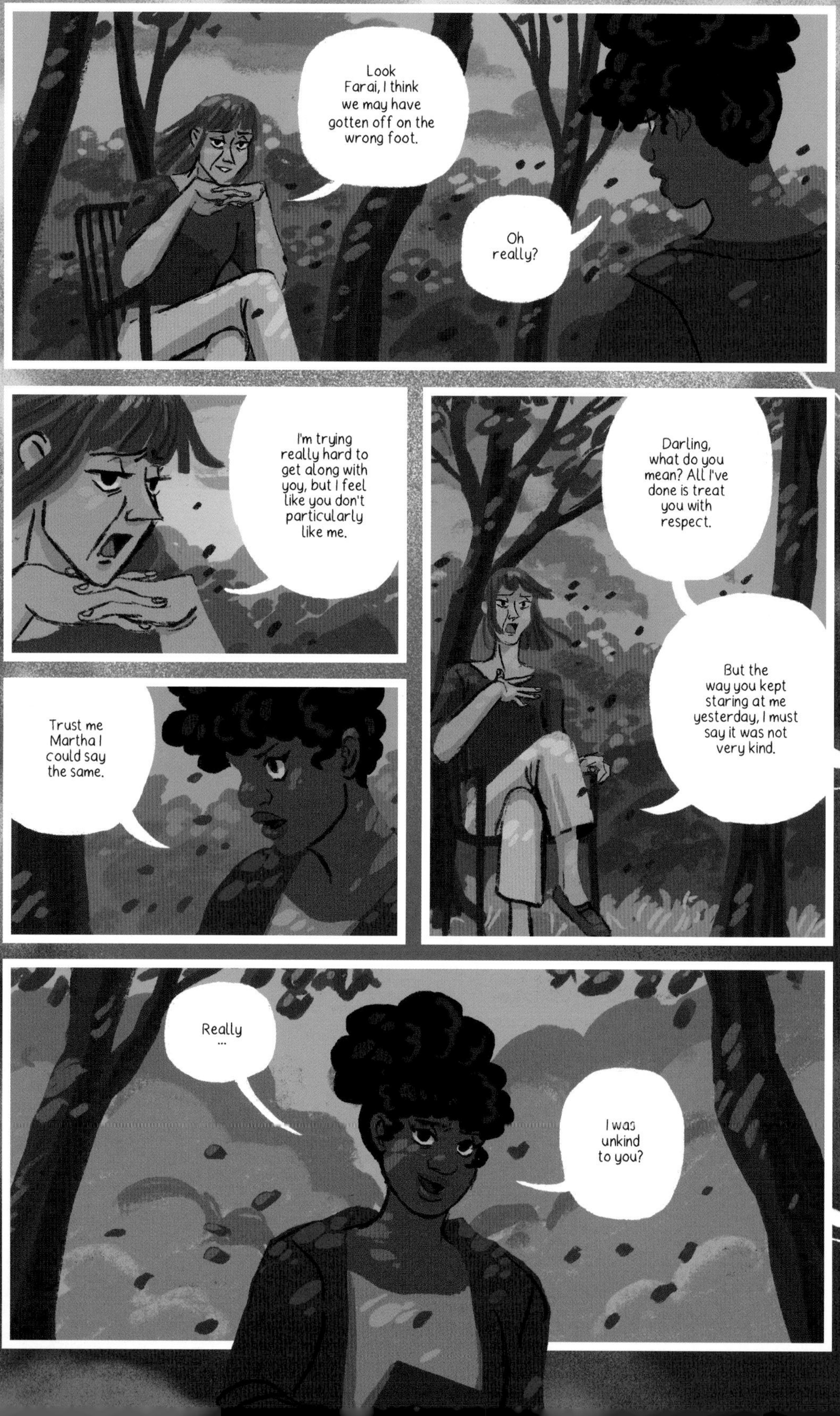
Look Farai, I think we may have gotten off on the wrong foot.
Oh really?
I'm trying really hard to get along with you, but I feel like you don't particularly like me.
Trust me Martha I could say the same.
Darling, what do you mean? All I've done is treat you with respect.
But the way you kept staring at me yesterday, I must say it was not very kind.
Really ...
I was unkind to you?

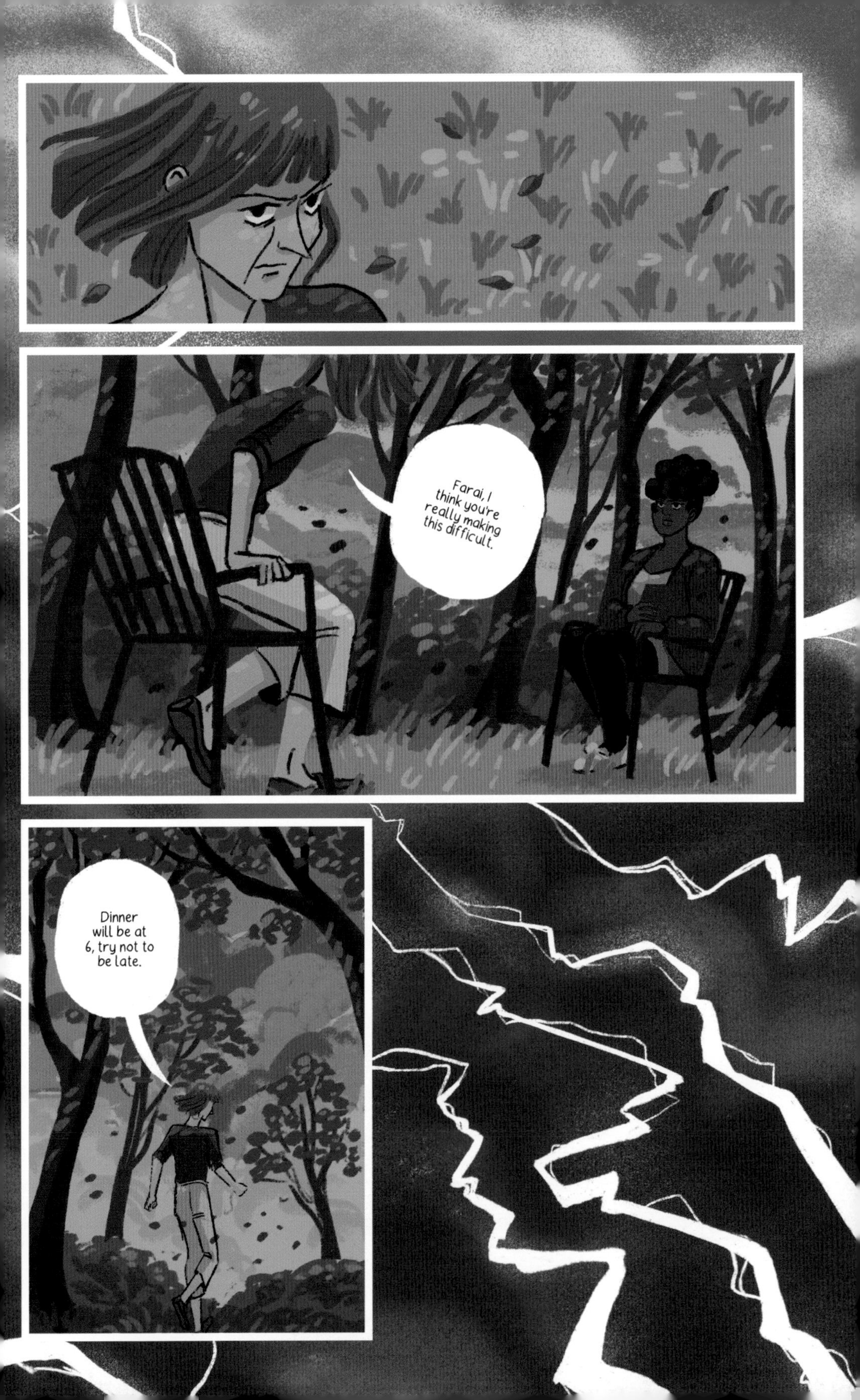
Farai, I think you're really making this difficult.
Dinner will be at 6, try not to be late.

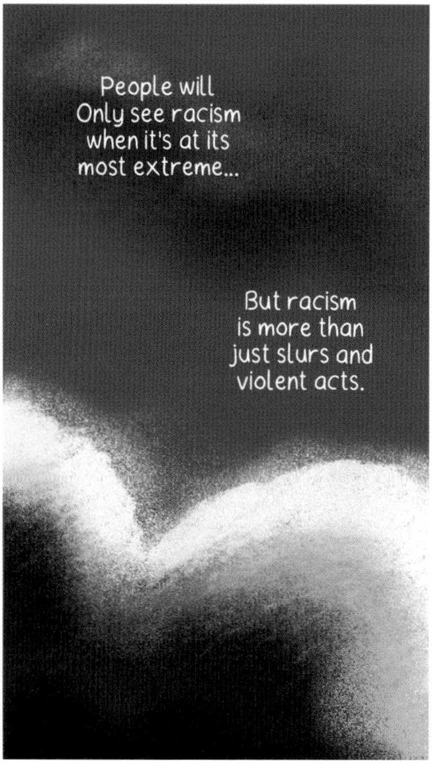
People will Only see racism when it's at its most extreme...
But racism is more than just slurs and violent acts.

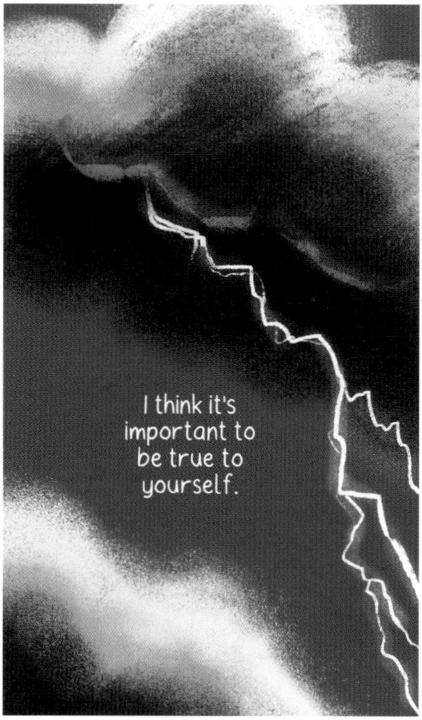
I think it's important to be true to yourself.

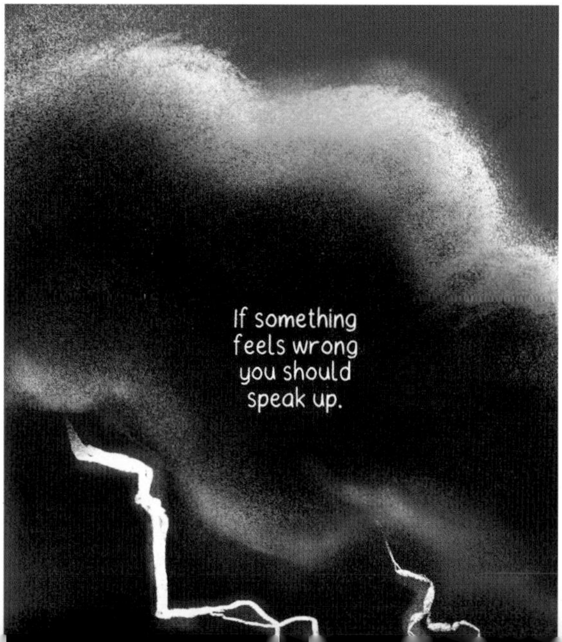
If something feels wrong you should speak up.

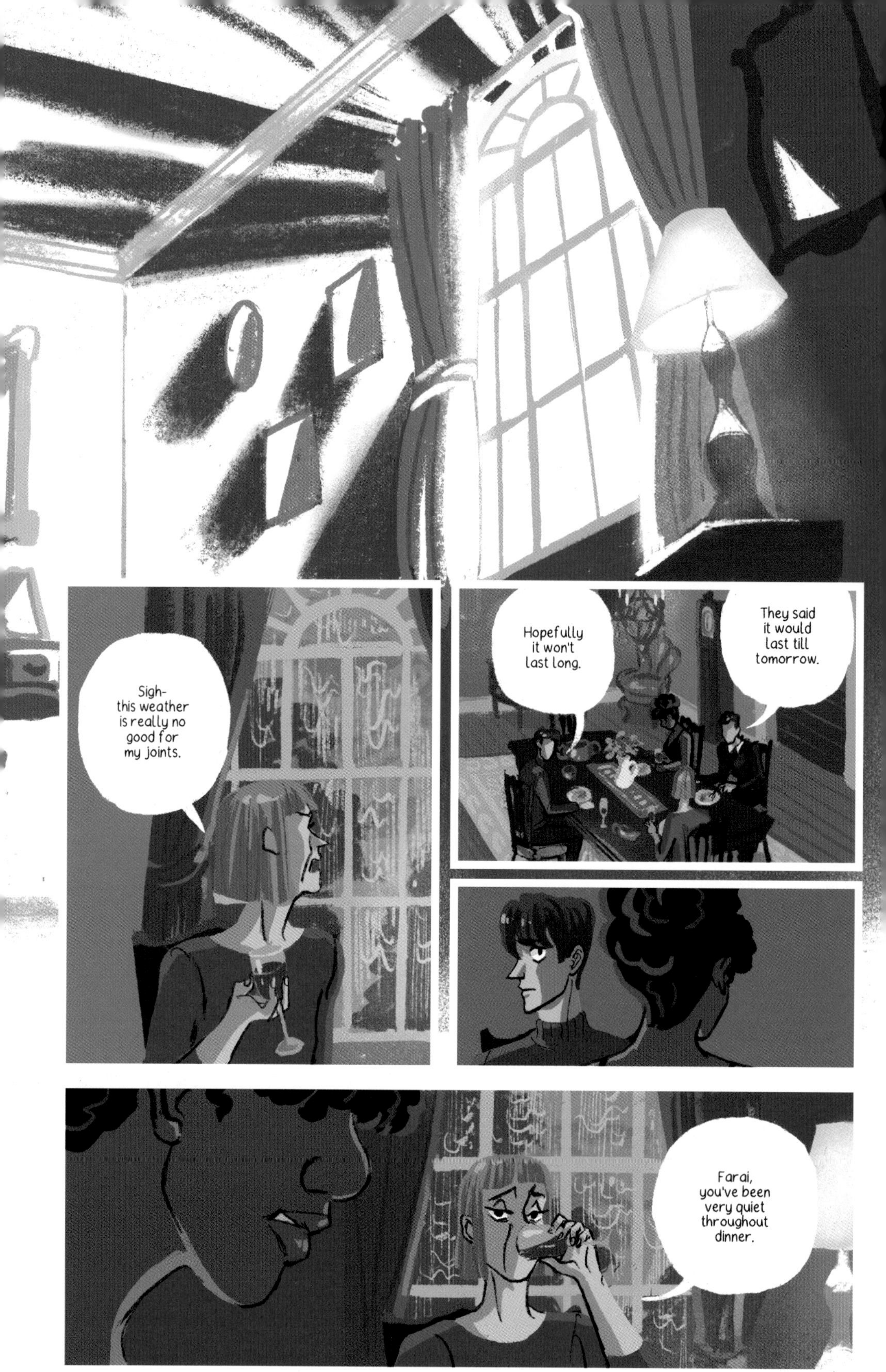
Sigh- this weather is really no good for my joints.
Hopefully it won't last long.
They said it would last till tomorrow.
Farai, you've been very quiet throughout dinner.

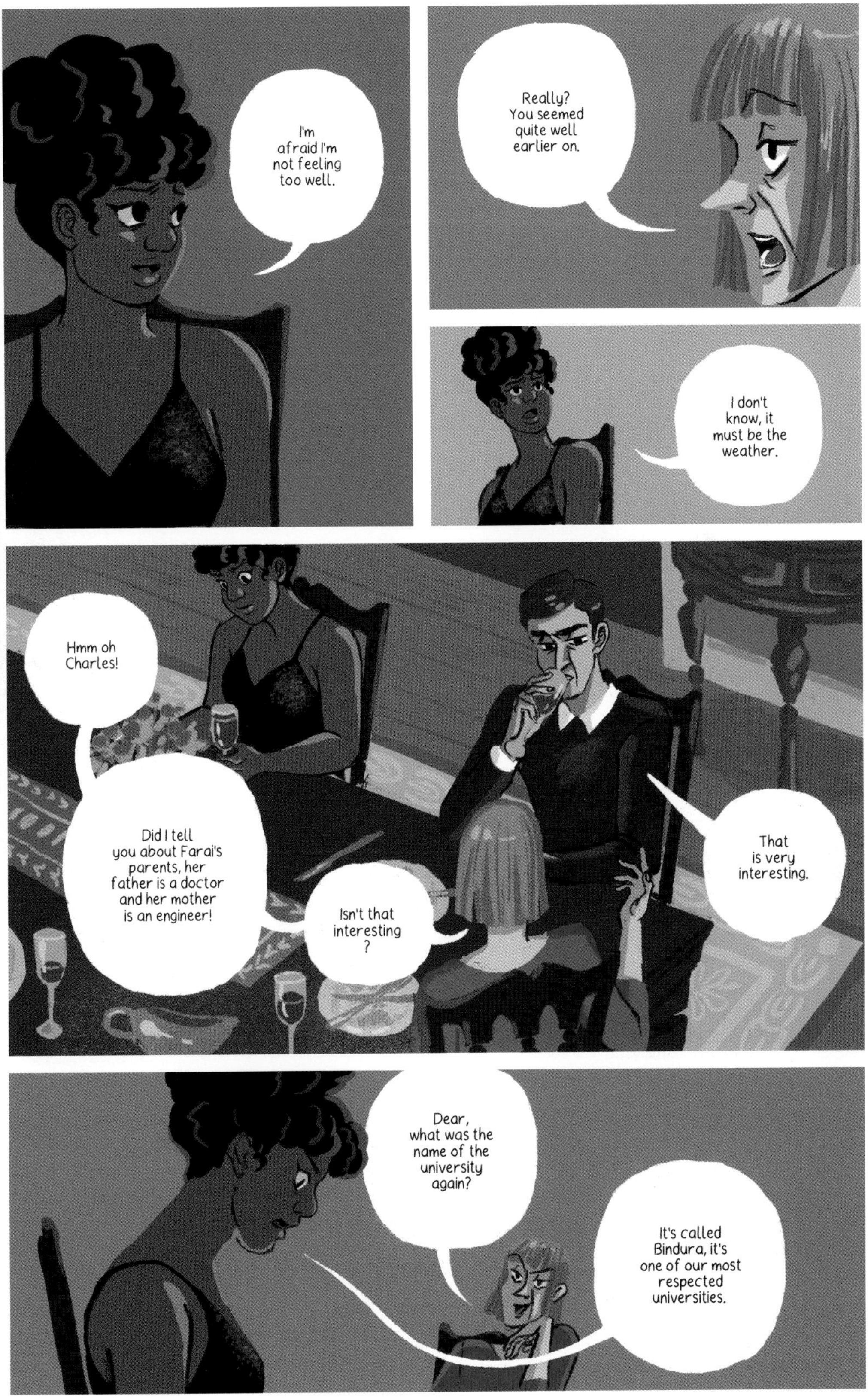
I'm afraid I'm not feeling too well.
Really? You seemed quite well earlier on.
I don't know, it must be the weather.
Hmm oh Charles!
Did I tell you about Farai's parents, her father is a doctor and her mother is an engineer!
Isn't that interesting ?
That is very interesting.
Dear, what was the name of the university again?
It's called Bindura, it's one of our most respected universities.

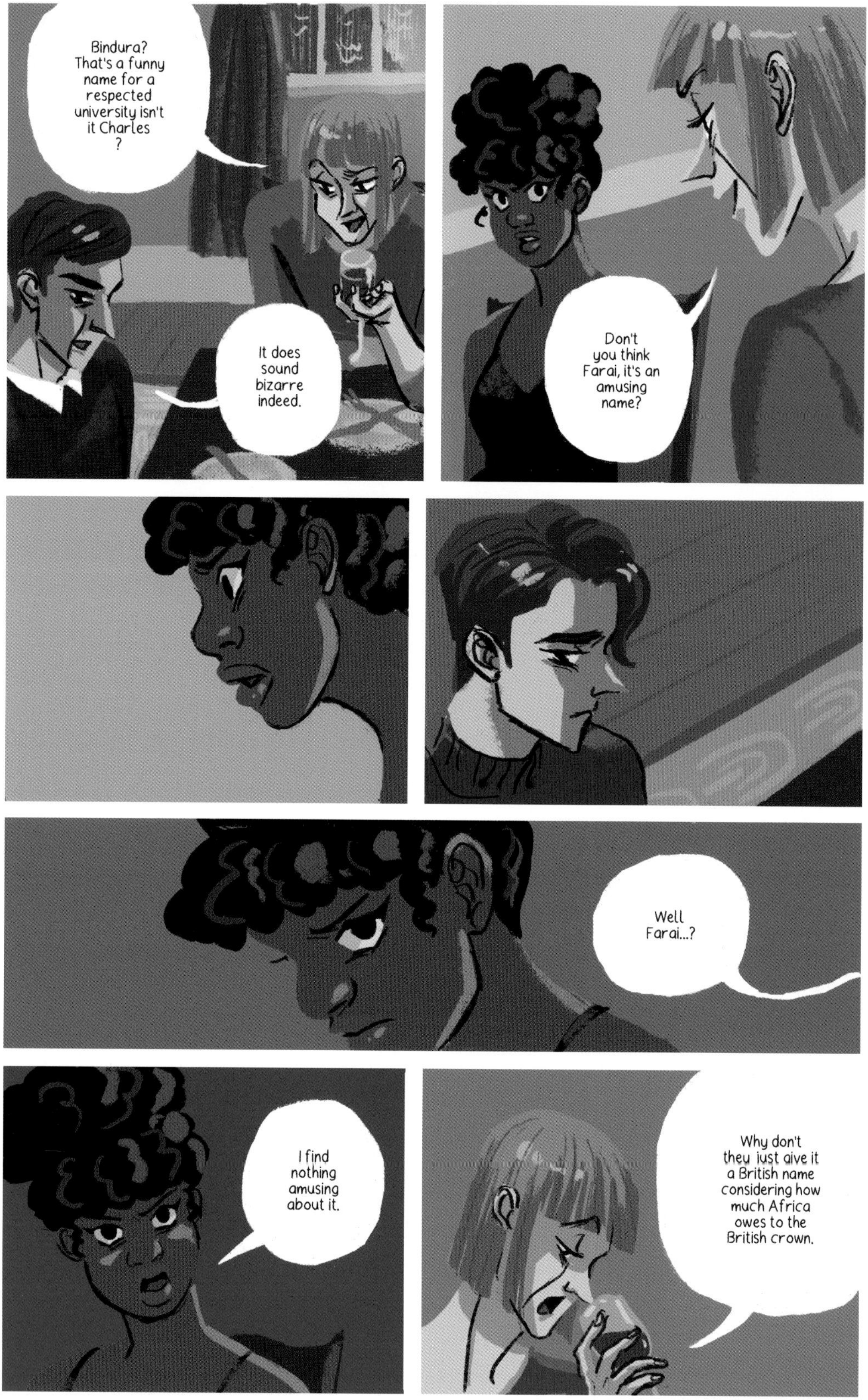
Bindura? That's a funny name for a respected university isn't it Charles ?
It does sound bizarre indeed.
Don't you think Farai, it's an amusing name?
Well Farai...?
I find nothing amusing about it.
Why don't they just give it a British name considering how much Africa owes to the British crown.

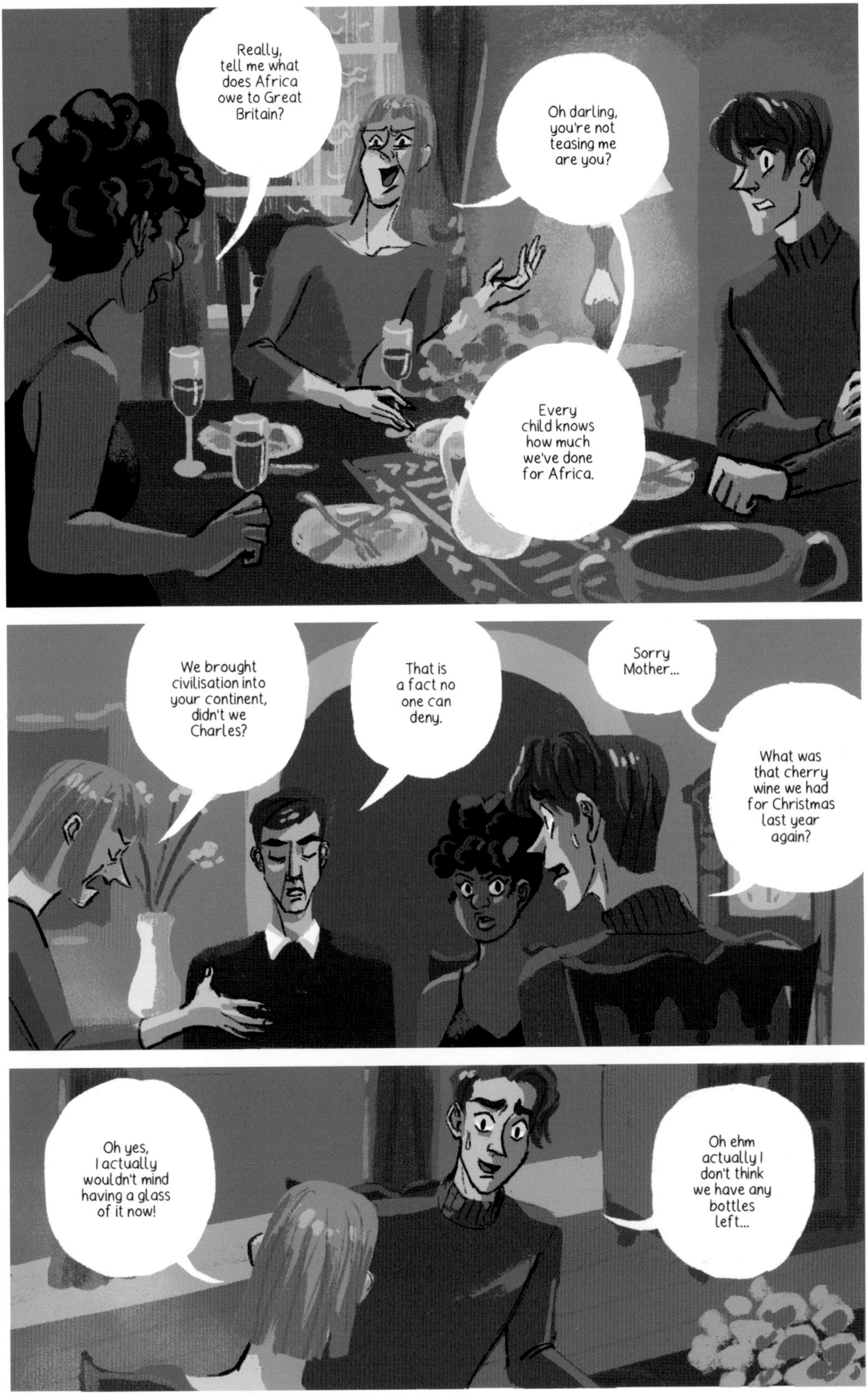

Really, tell me what does Africa owe to Great Britain?
Oh darling, you're not teasing me are you?
Every child knows how much we've done for Africa.
We brought civilisation into your continent, didn't we Charles?
That is a fact no one can deny.
Sorry Mother...
What was that cherry wine we had for Christmas last year again?
Oh yes, I actually wouldn't mind having a glass of it now!
Oh ehm actually I don't think we have any bottles left...

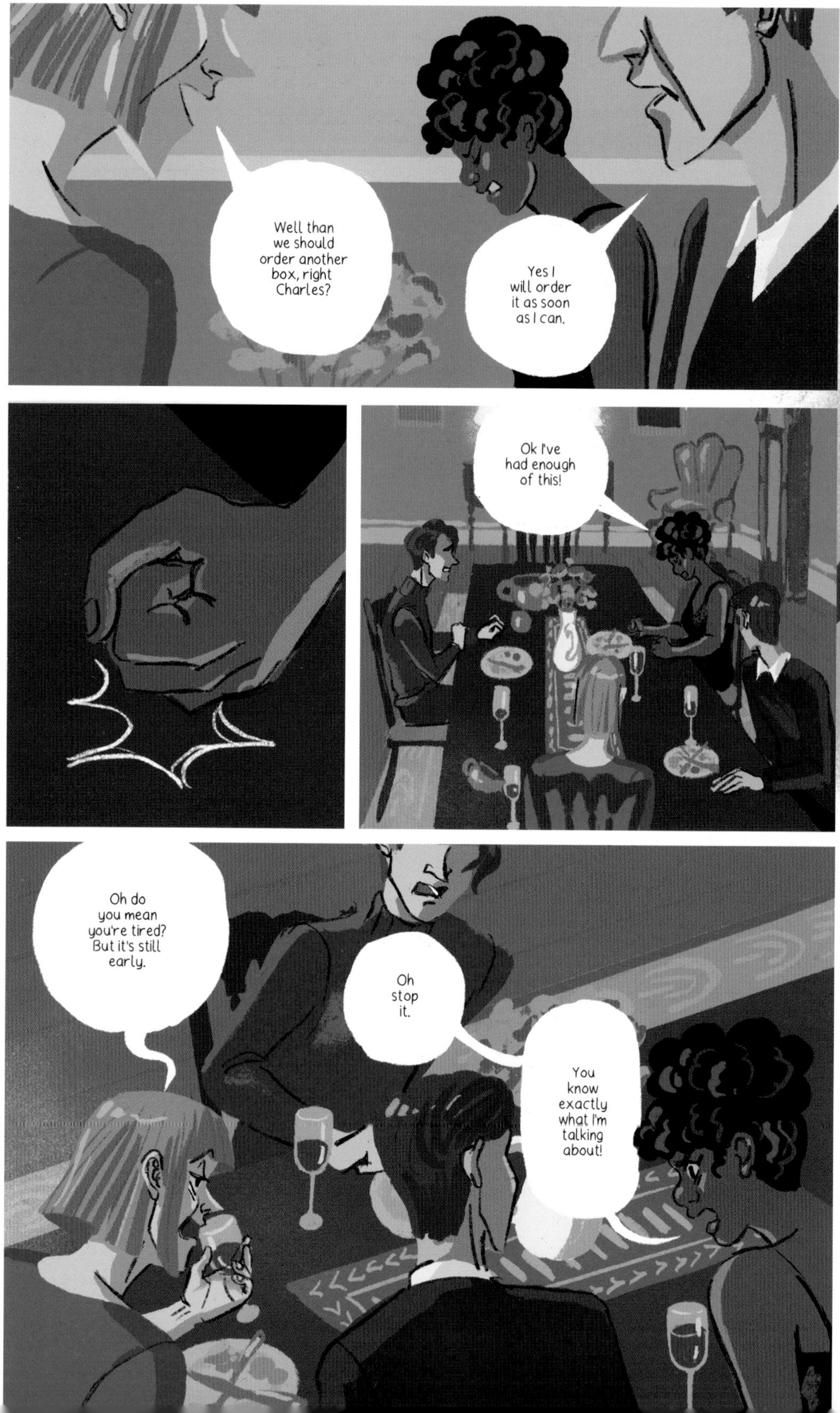
Well than we should order another box, right Charles?
Yes I will order it as soon as I can.
Ok I've had enough of this!
Oh do you mean you're tired? But it's still early.
Oh stop it.
You know exactly what I'm talking about!

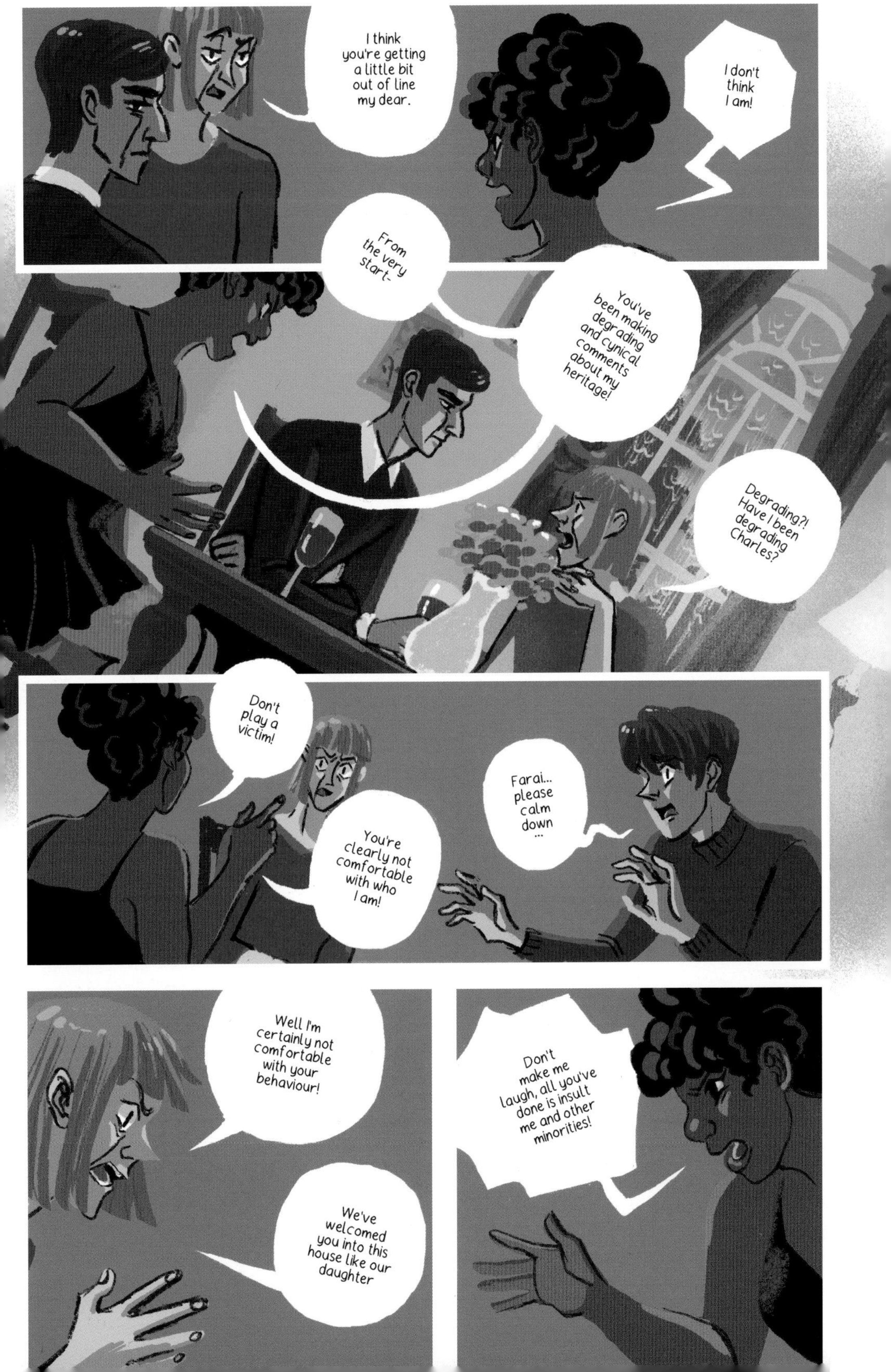
I think you're getting a little bit out of line my dear.
I don't think I am!
From the very start-
You've been making degrading and cynical comments about my heritage!
Degrading?! Have I been degrading Charles?
Don't play a victim!
You're clearly not comfortable with who I am!
Farai... please calm down ...
Well I'm certainly not comfortable with your behaviour!
We've welcomed you into this house like our daughter
Don't make me laugh, all you've done is insult me and other minorities!

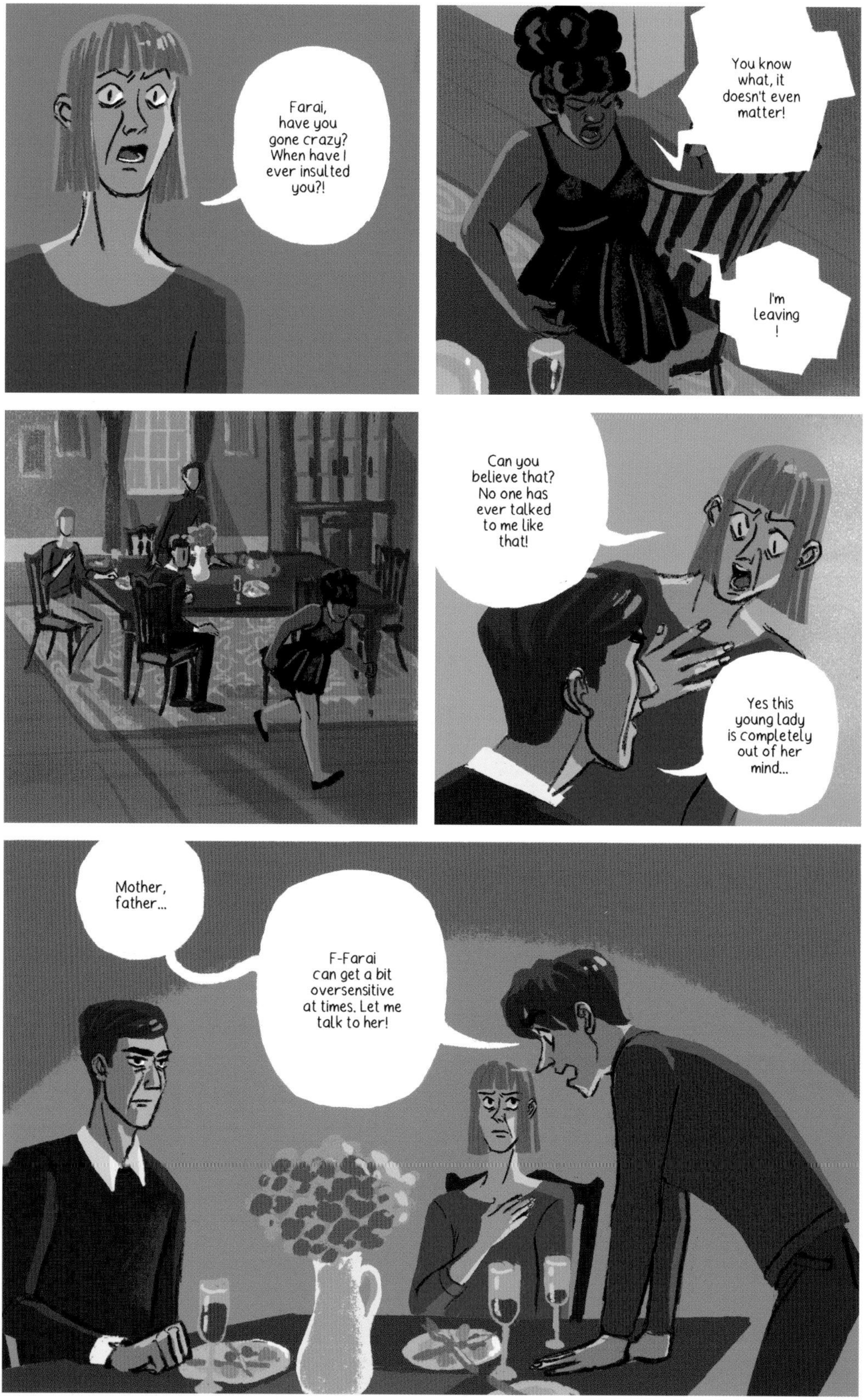
Farai, have you gone crazy? When have I ever insulted you?!
You know what, it doesn't even matter!
I'm leaving !
Can you believe that? No one has ever talked to me like that!
Yes this young lady is completely out of her mind...
Mother, father...
F-Farai can get a bit oversensitive at times. Let me talk to her!

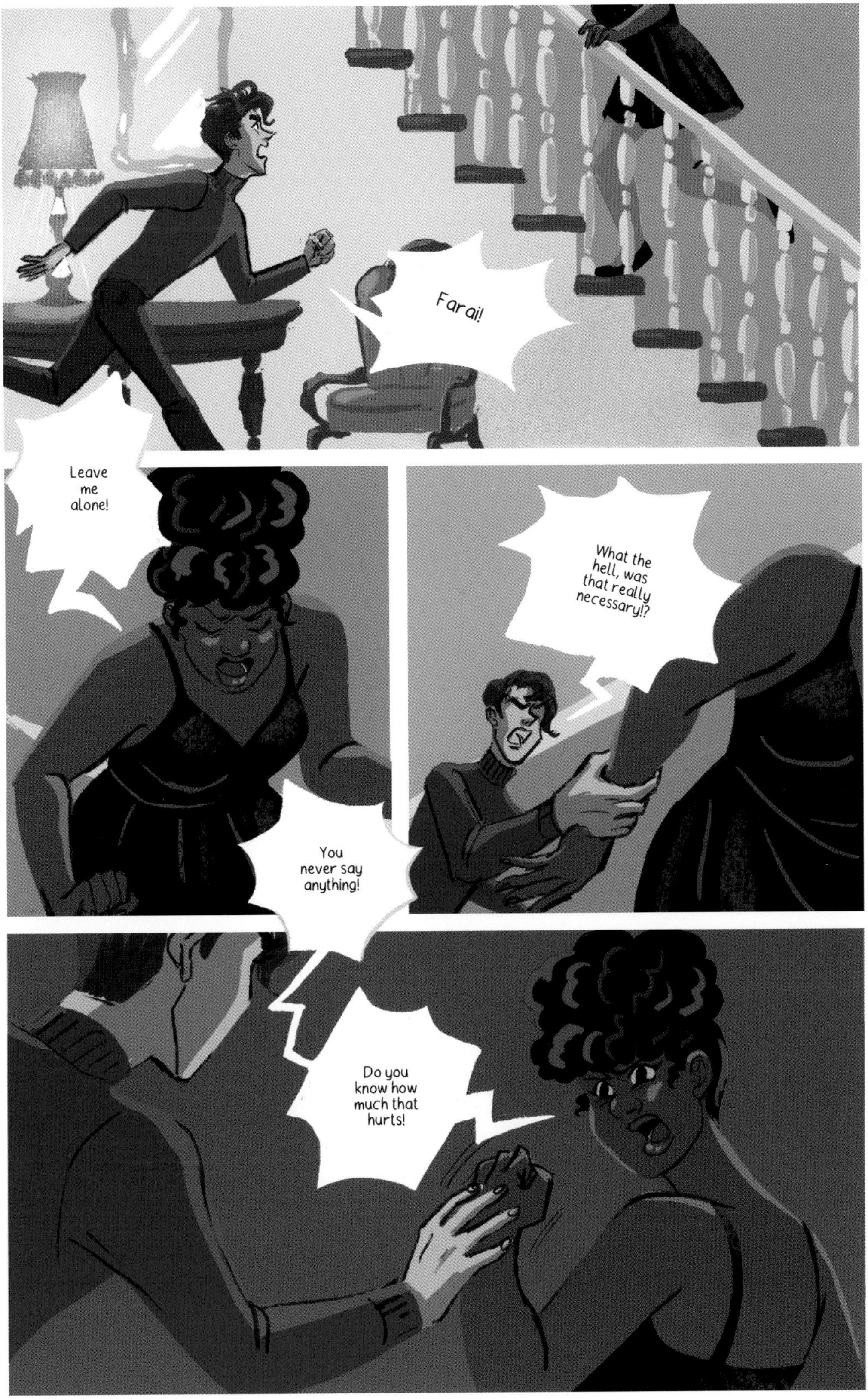
Farai!
Leave me alone!
What the hell, was that really necessary!?
You never say anything!
Do you know how much that hurts!

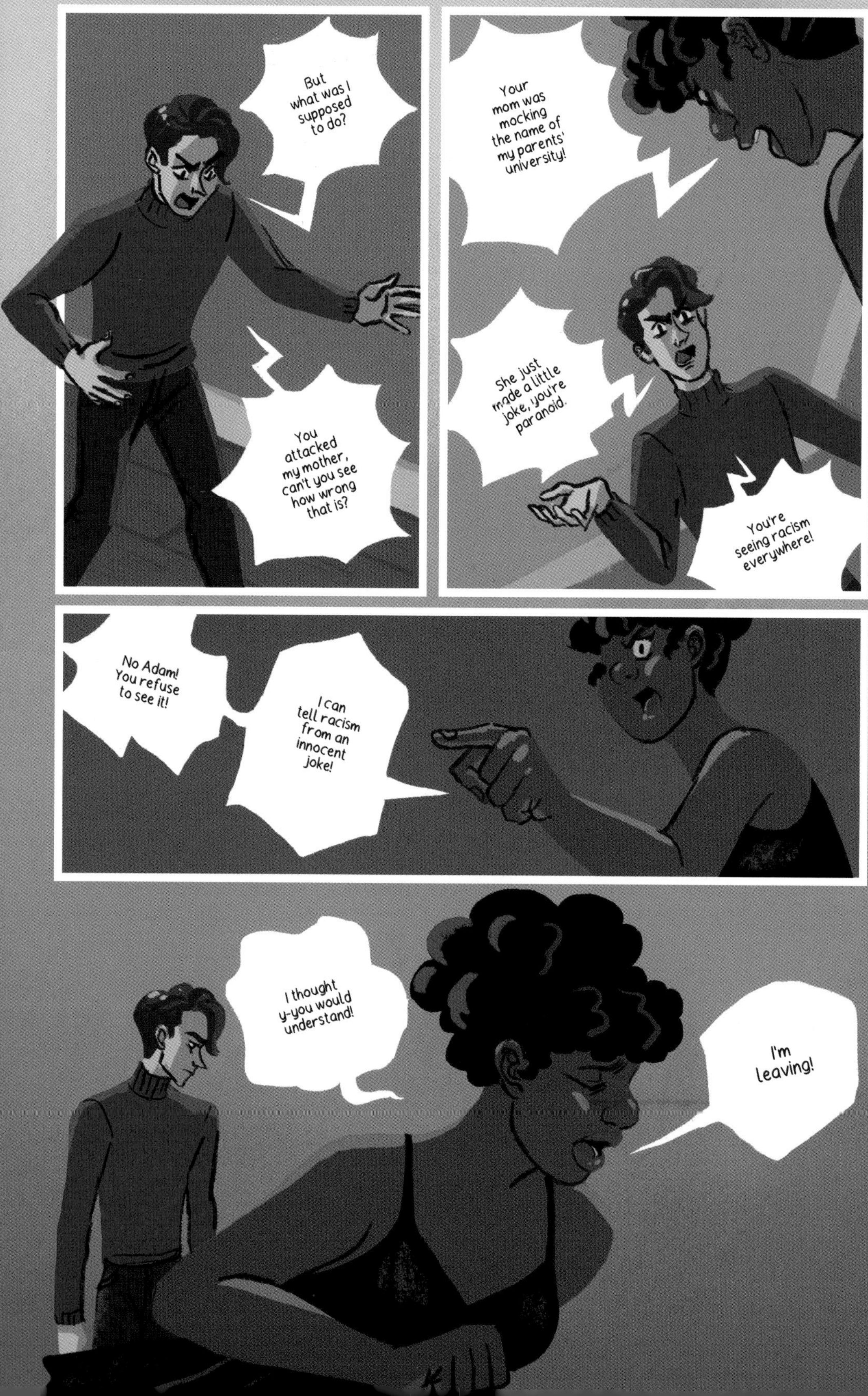
But what was I supposed to do?
You attacked my mother, can't you see how wrong that is?
Your mom was mocking the name of my parents' university!
She just made a little joke, you're paranoid.
You're seeing racism everywhere!
No Adam! You refuse to see it!
I can tell racism from an innocent joke!
I thought y-you would understand!
I'm leaving!

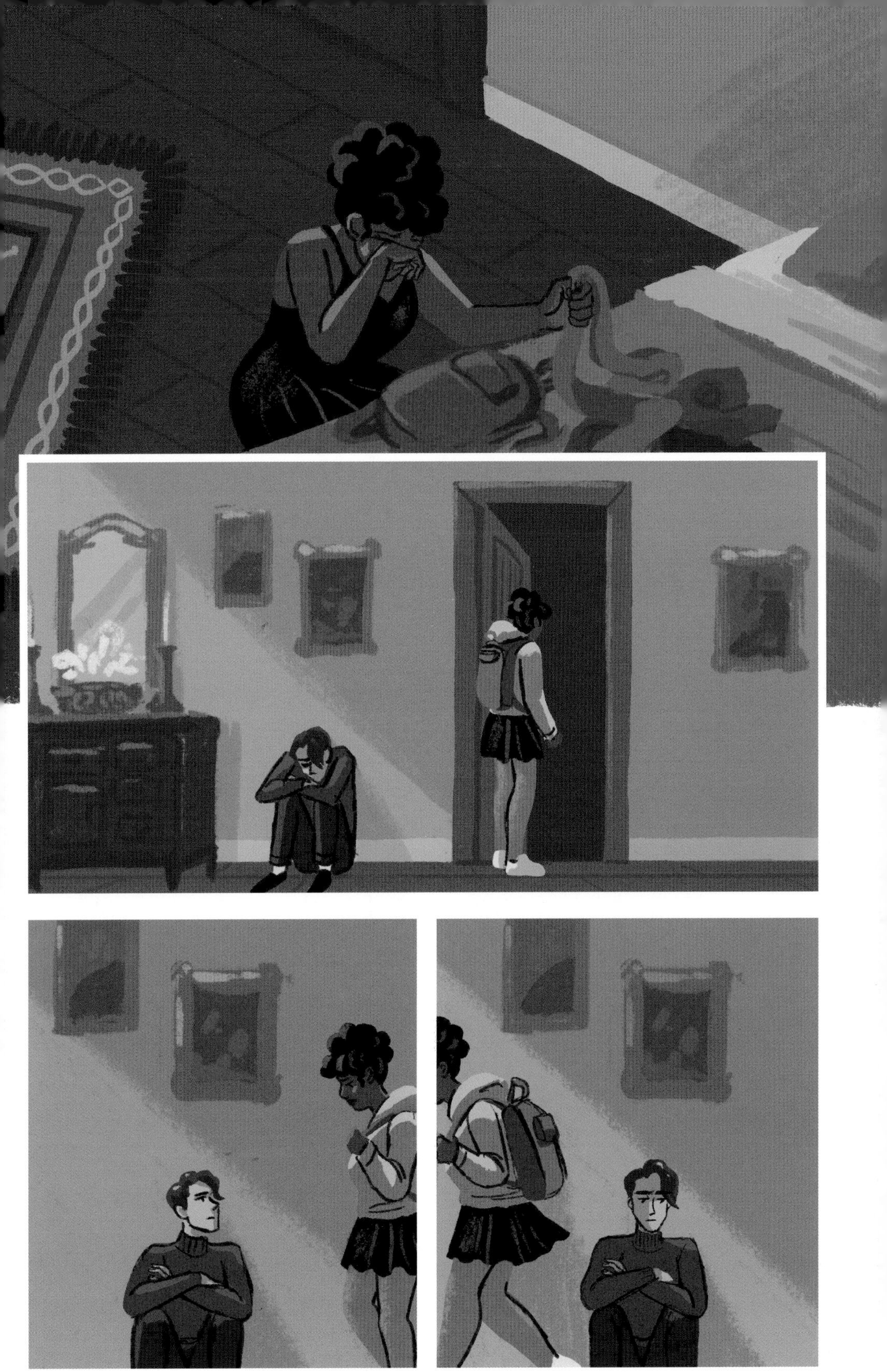

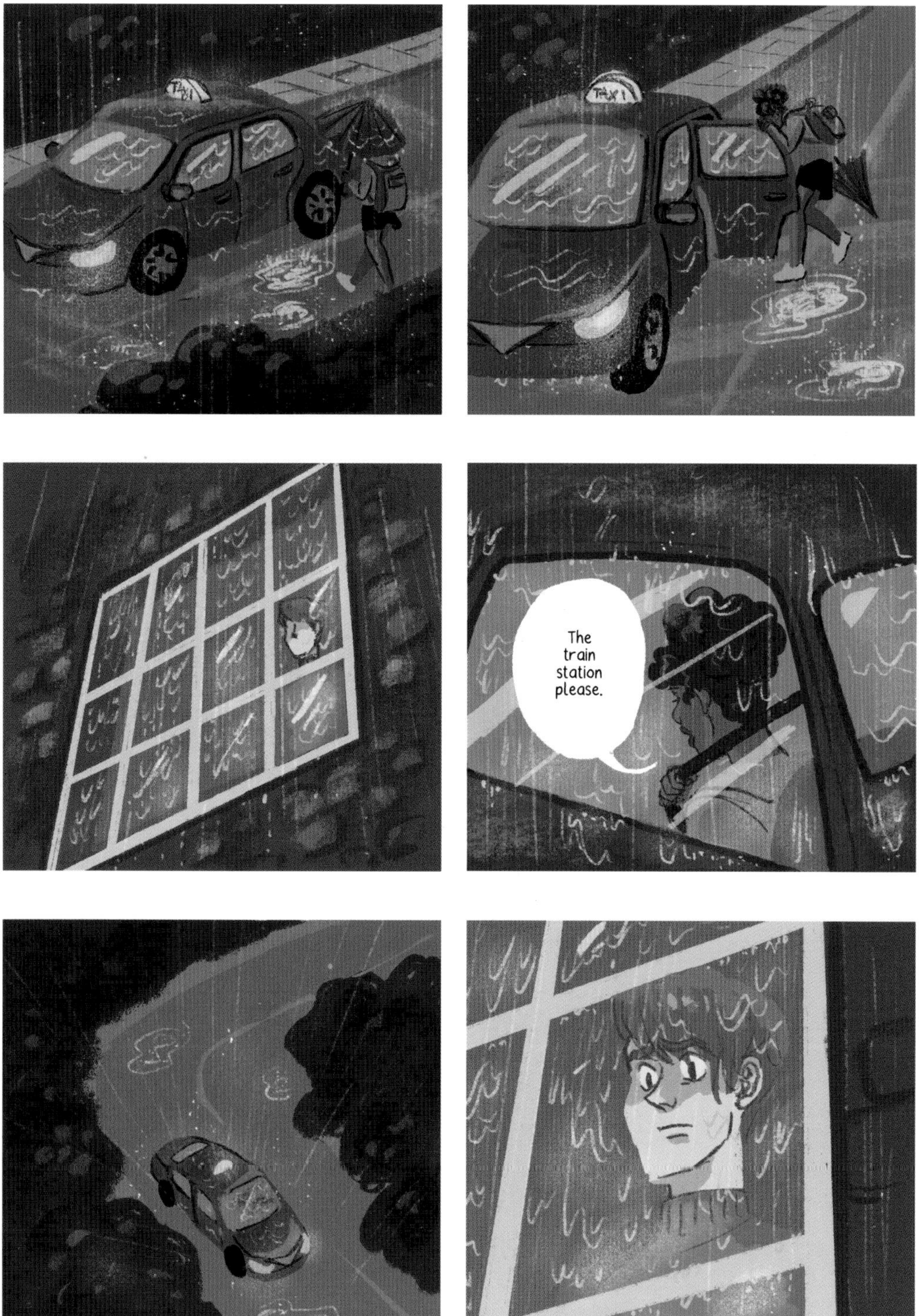
The train station please.

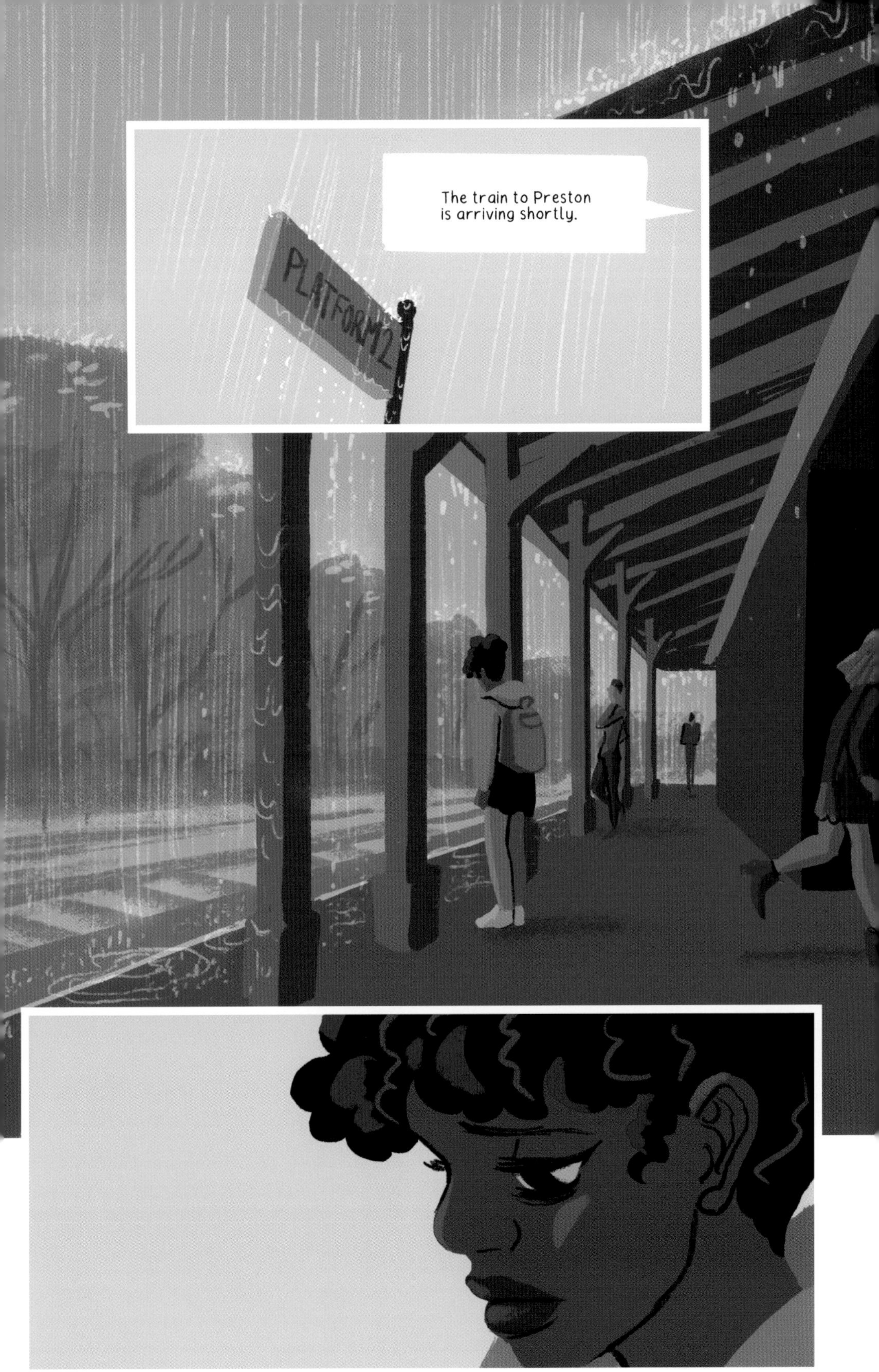
The train to Preston is arriving shortly.
PLATFORM 2

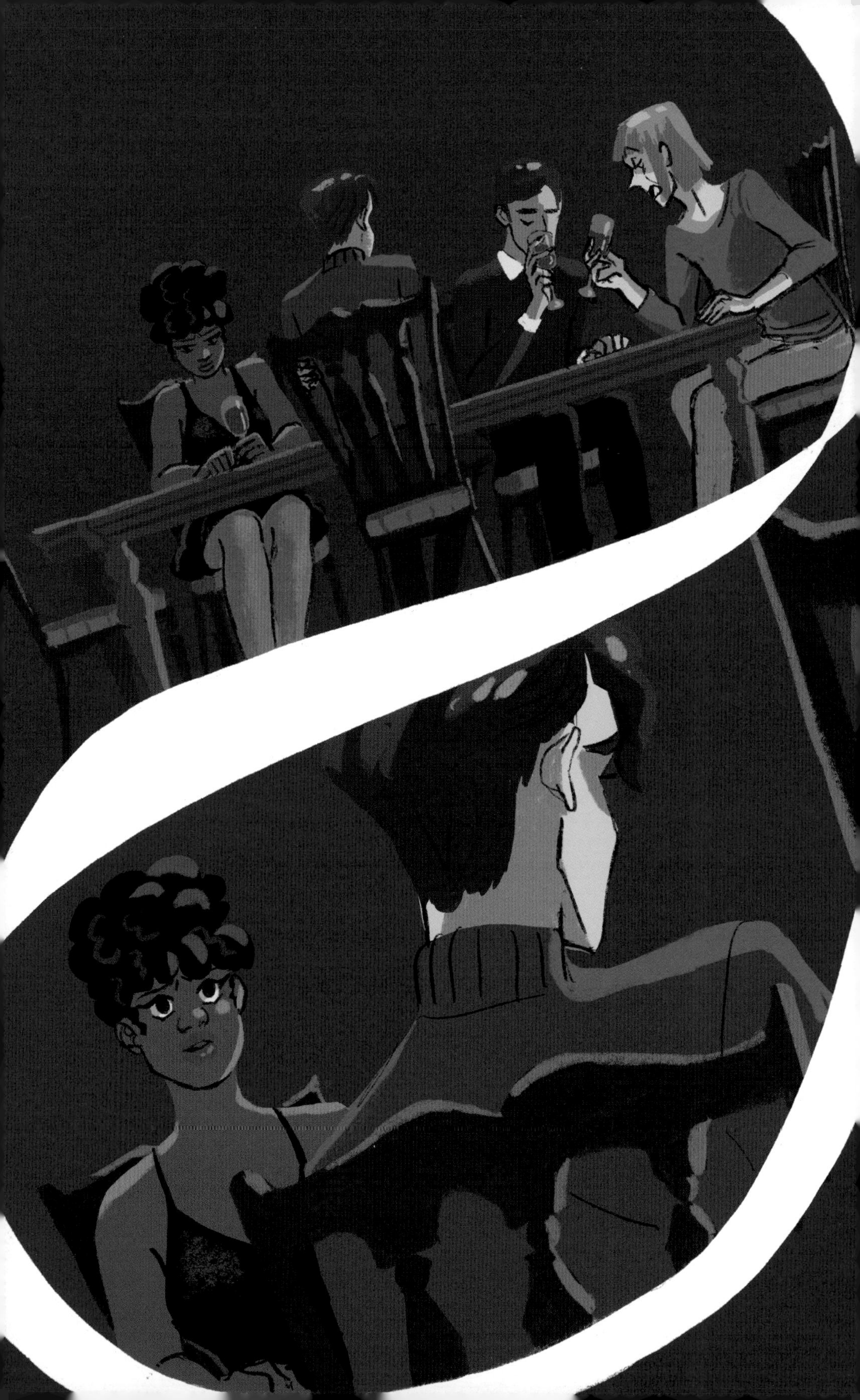

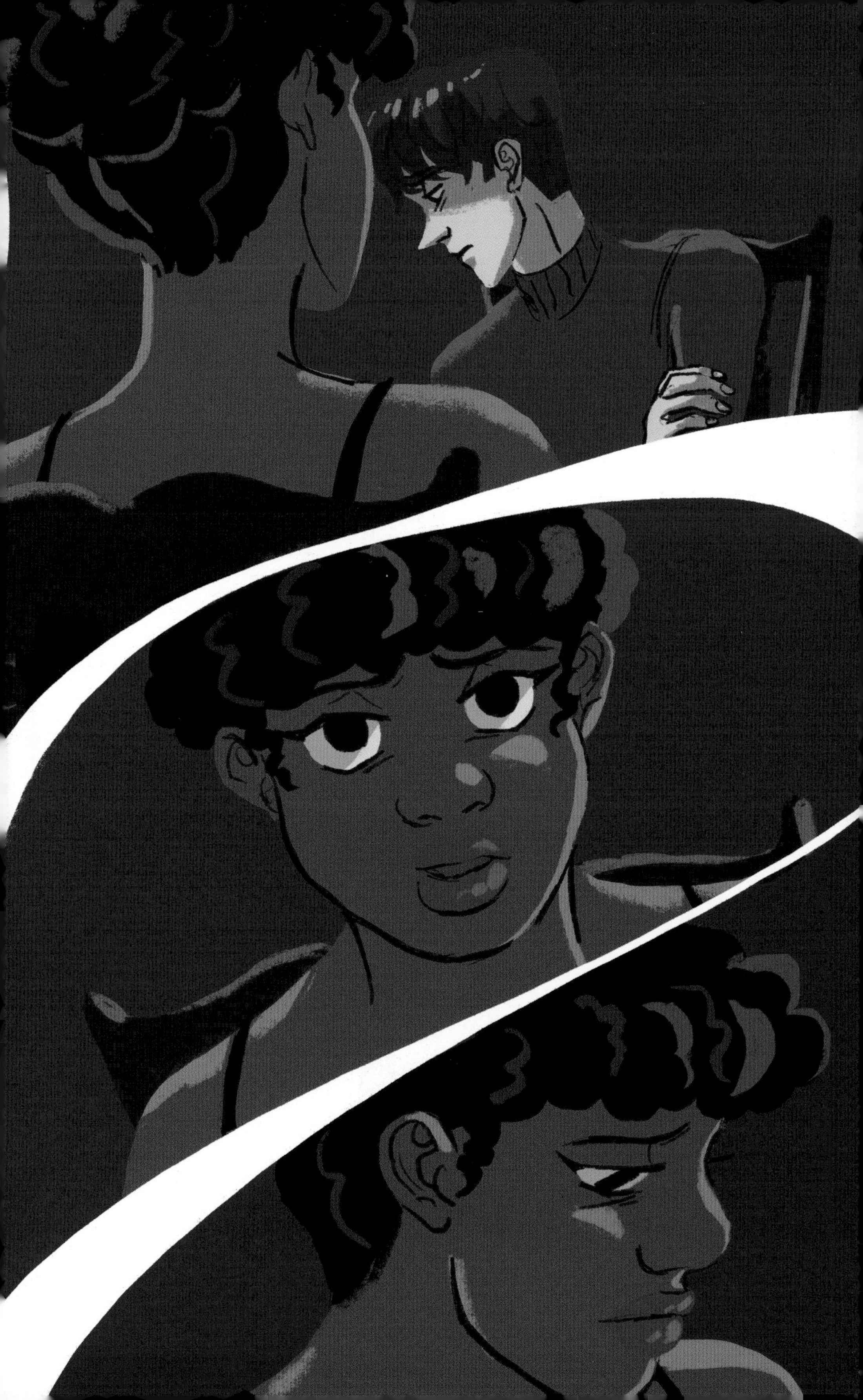

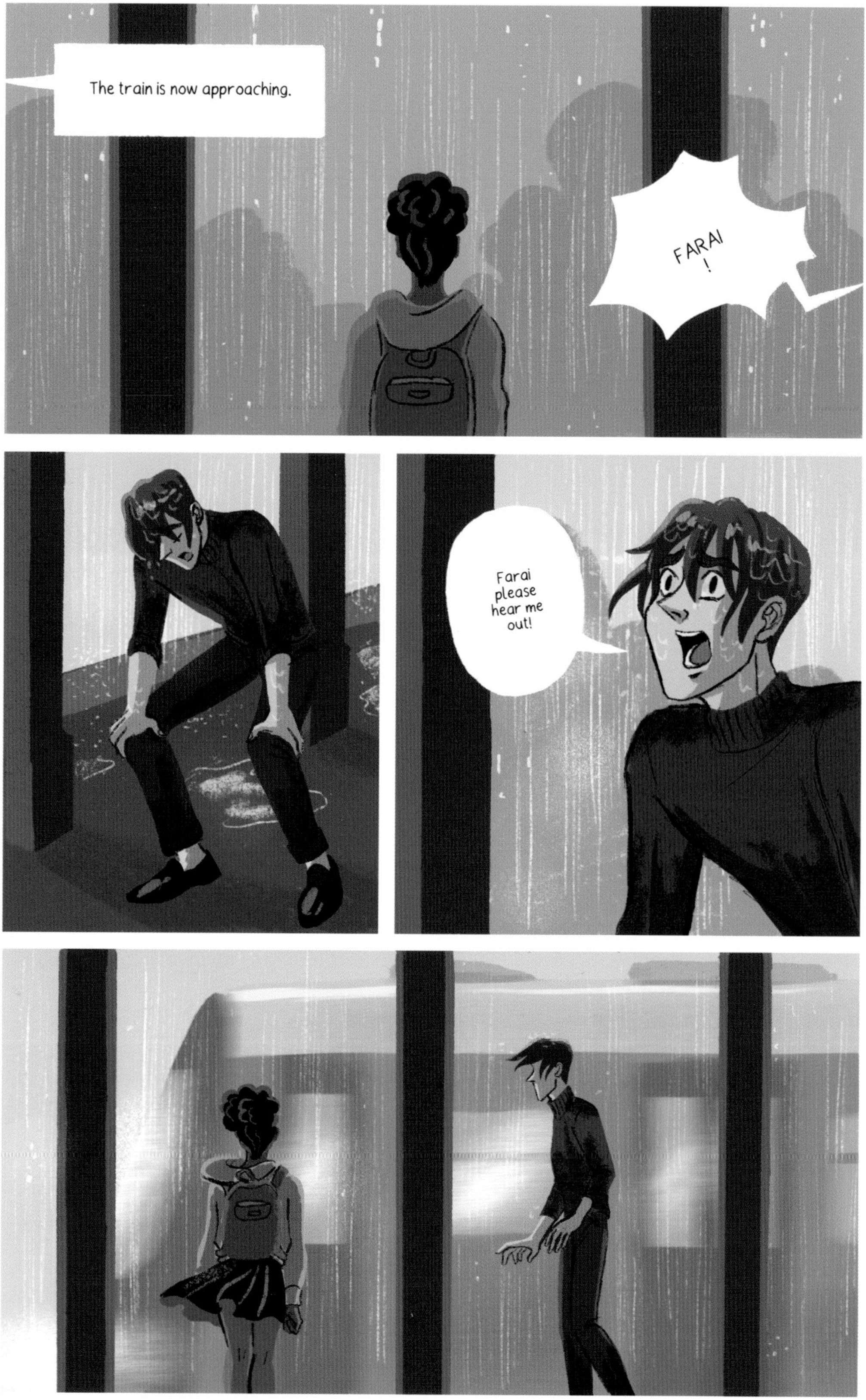
The train is now approaching.
FARAI!
Farai please hear me out!

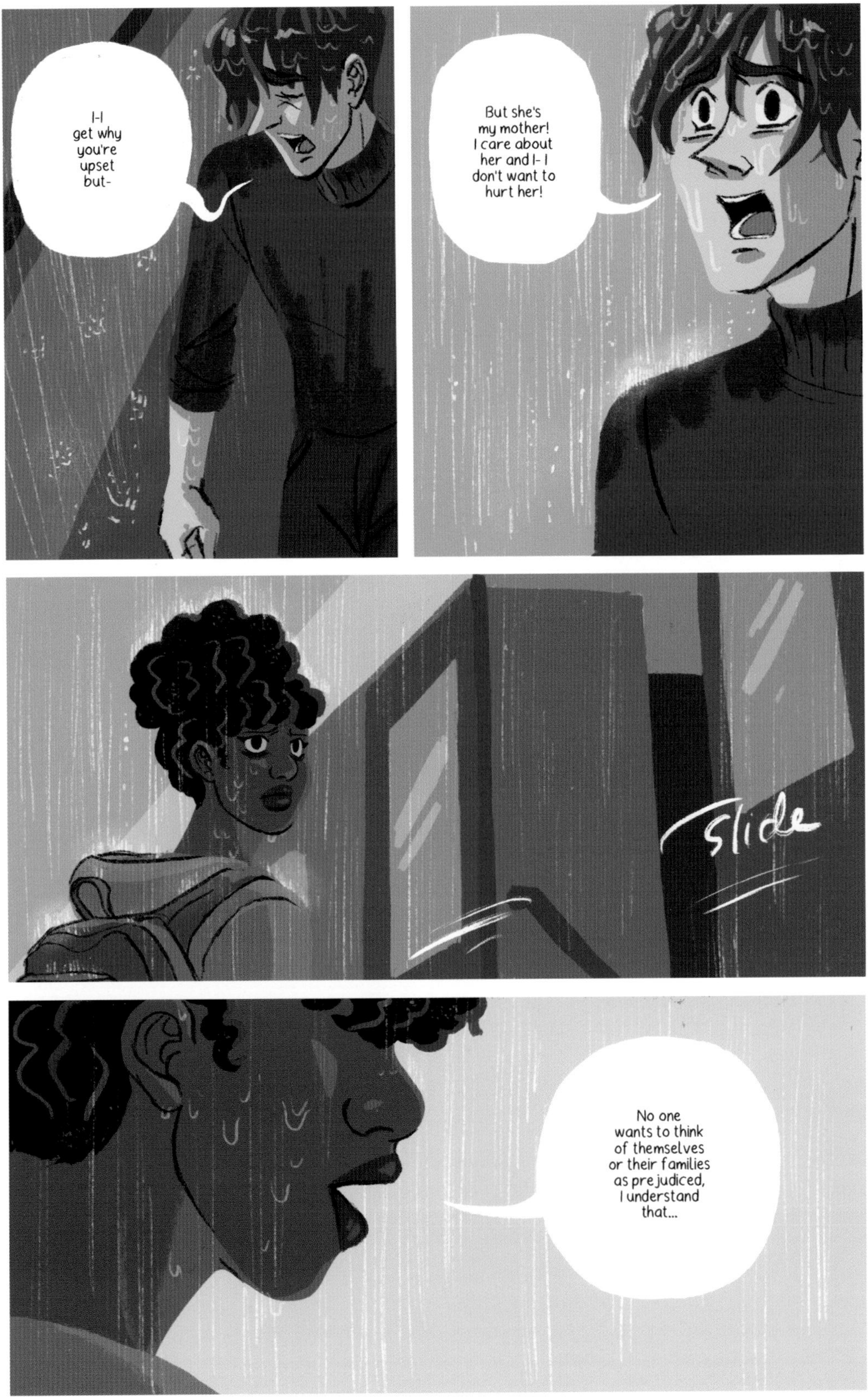
I-I get why you're upset but-
But she's my mother! I care about her and I- I don't want to hurt her!
slide
No one wants to think of themselves or their families as prejudiced, I understand that...

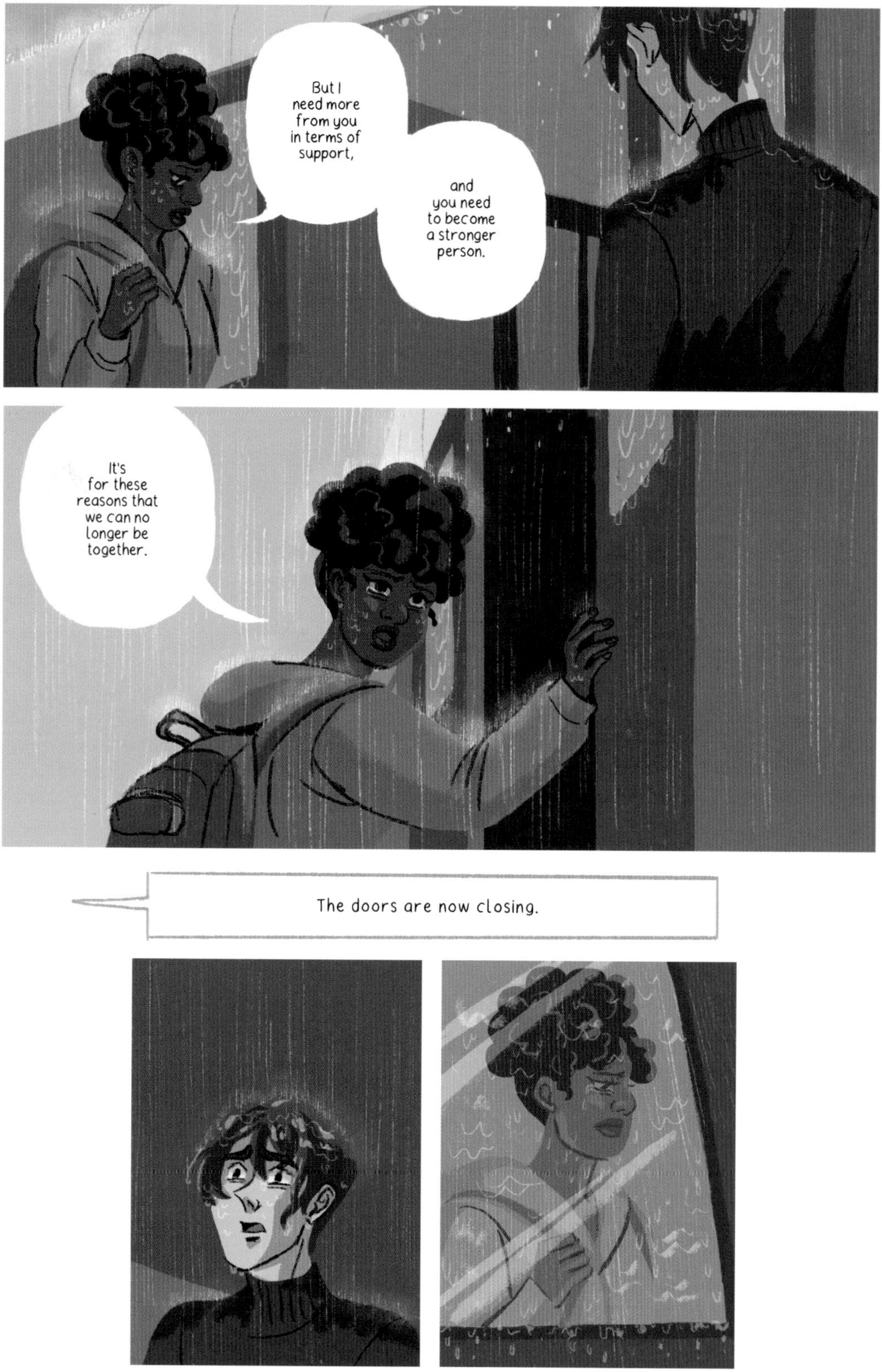
But I need more from you in terms of support,
and you need to become a stronger person.
It's for these reasons that we can no longer be together.
The doors are now closing.

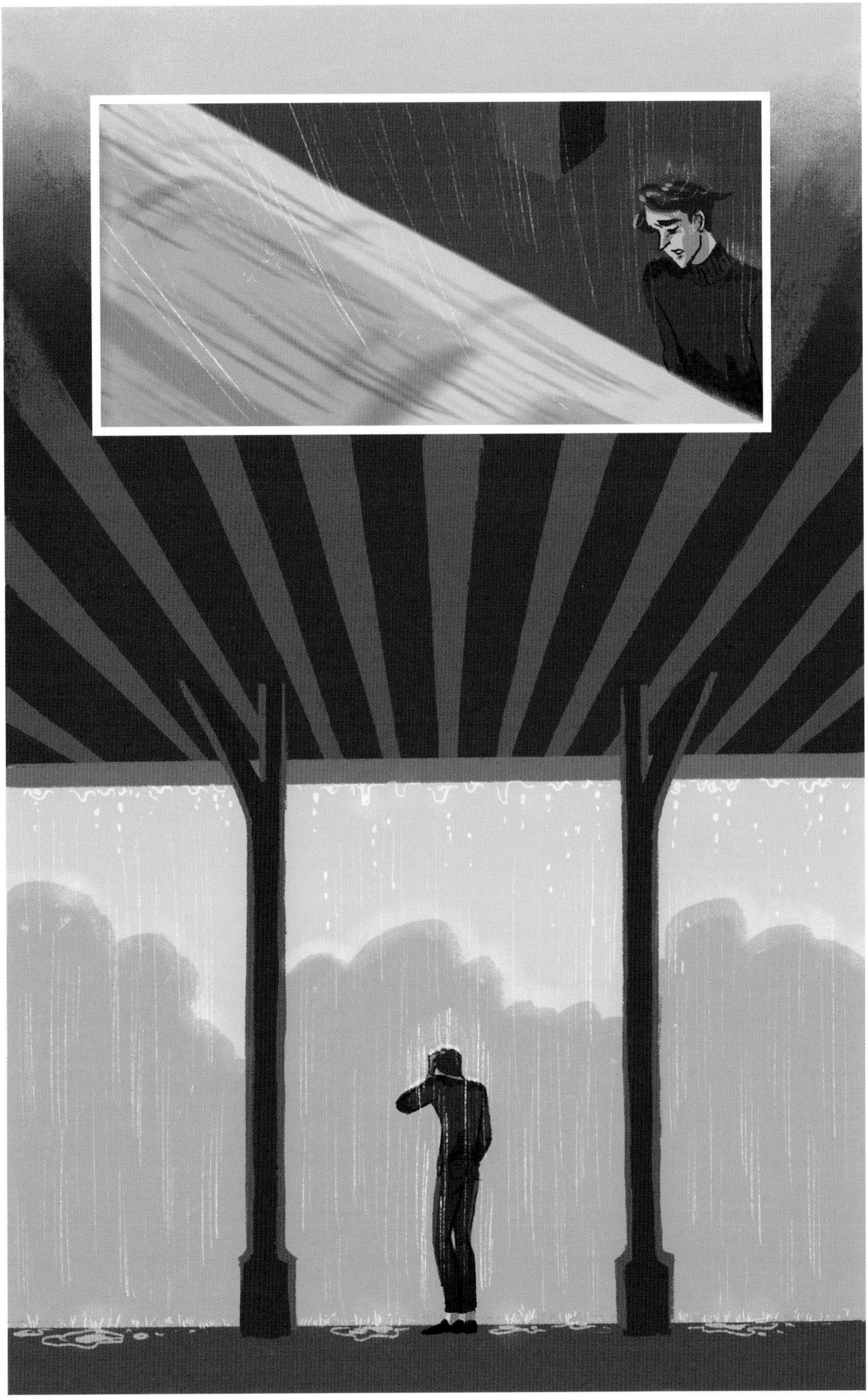

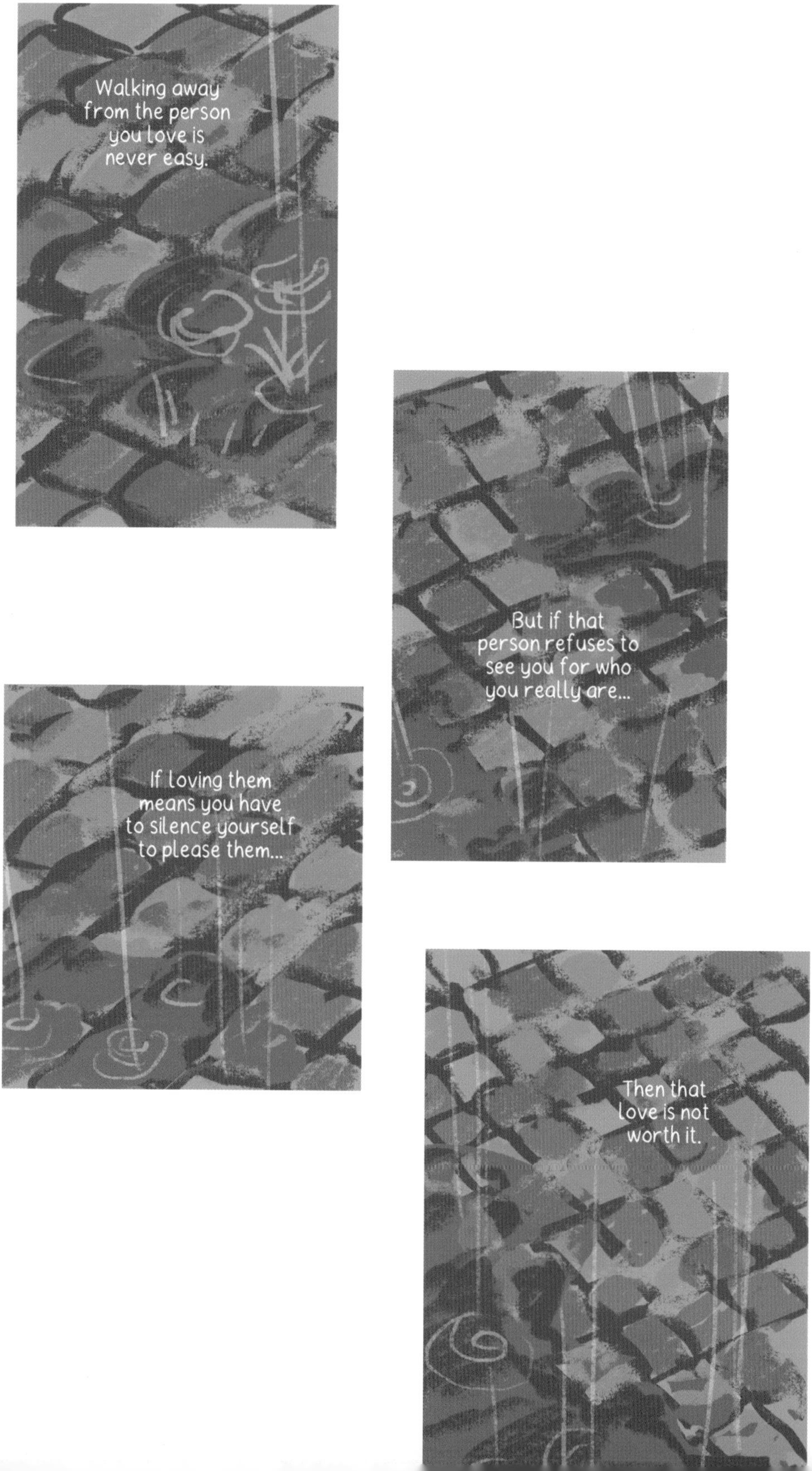
Walking away from the person you love is never easy.
But if that person refuses to see you for who you really are...
If loving them means you have to silence yourself to please them...
Then that love is not worth it.

ACKNOWLEDGEMENTS

I would like to thank my partner Jacek who basically brainstormed the idea with me and helped me write out the script, and for literally acting out the dialogue with me! You've always believed in me and pushed me to do my best and I'm grateful to have you in my life.

Seánie, my assistant, who willingly jumped in to help when I thought I wasn't going to make it, you were a true hero and I couldn't have done it without you!

Alex and Shazleen, for your endless emotional support. Every time I felt trapped and stressed out you were always there to listen. Thank you for cheering me on and believing in me.

Ricky, for being so patient, for sharing your knowledge with me and helping me shape a story I can be proud of.

-Charlot Kristensen

Published by Avery Hill Publishing, 2020

10 9 8 7 6 5 4 3 2 1

First published in the UK in 2020 by
Avery Hill Publishing
Unit 8
5 Durham Yard
London
E2 6QF

A CIP record for this book is available from the British Library

ISBN: 978-1-910395-55-4

Charlot Kristensen
www.charlotkristensen.com

Avery Hill Publishing
www.averyhillpublishing.com